# BLACK FAIRY

## and other plays for children

## Useni Eugene Perkins

**also by Useni Eugene Perkins . . .**

for children:
*The Afrocentric Self-Inventory and Discovery Workbook*

for adults:
*Harvesting New Generations: The Positive Development of Black
    Youth*
*Home Is a Dirty Street: The Social Oppression of Black Children*
*Explosion of Chicago's Black Street Gangs: 1900 to Present*

THIRD  WORLD  PRESS

# BLACK FAIRY

## and other plays for children

### Useni Eugene Perkins

### Third World Press
### Chicago

**BLACK FAIRY AND OTHER PLAYS FOR CHILDREN**

First Edition 1993
First Printing 1993
ISBN: 0-88378-077-1
Library of Congress #: 92-60054

cover and inside illustrations by Patrick Hill
cover and title pages designed by Craig Taylor

Manufactured in the United States of America.
Third World Press
P.O. Box 19730
Chicago, IL 60619

**TO MY CHILDREN –**

*Julia Evalyn and Russell Patrice,*
*and also to Jamila Saran*

# CONTENTS

# CONTENTS

# FOREWORD

Over the past twenty five years, my destiny has been intertwined with Useni Eugene Perkins as we developed our consciousness and commitment to the African-American community. Useni cares deeply for our children and has had a profound effect upon the choices I have made to develop a cultural institution that would make a difference for them.

As a social work practitioner, Useni has done yeoman work in his writing to help us more fully understand the young Black male in particular. Through his scholarship in two best selling books, *Home is a Dirty Street* and *Harvesting New Generations* and his numerous consultations and essays, our knowledge of how to protect and advance the development of the young Black male has taken a quantum leap. An outstanding poet as well, Useni's poem "Hey, Black Child" salutes and challenges our children to be all that they can be and has been nationally distributed in poster form.

Useni's plays, written expressly for children, add another dimension to his commitment to mirror heroic images for us to emulate. "Black Fairy" is a classic unequaled in literature. "Young John Henry" and "The Legend of Deadwood Dick" lift up legendary heroes while emphasizing important values. These plays stress African-American people's infinite capacity to achieve once our glorious history is internalized and accepted as a paradigm for continued excellence.

Since 1985, ETA Creative Arts Foundation has produced Useni's plays in repertory. Over the years, more than 70,000 children have come with their teachers from the public schools, Head Start programs and day care centers to see his plays. When they leave, their eyes are shining, they are quoting lines from the plays, and they know, once and for all, that African Americans have their own resounding voice. Children often send us letters detailing the meaning that the experience had for them. They'll even draw characters from the play. Teachers also write to say how grateful they are that ETA is producing Useni's plays, which they find inspirational and helpful as they work with the children to incorporate African-centered values. The study guides that we prepare assist the teachers in reaching academic goals in language arts, spelling, geography and arithmetic. Many of the teachers also say that the history, which is embedded in each of Useni's scripts, is a lesson for them as well.

Many have quoted the ancient proverb, "Children are the reward of life." Useni's work gives those who want to bring action to these words a way to do it. And "doing it" is what it is all about at this stage of our history. As producers of live theater for young people, we are proud to share Useni's deep love for our children and demonstrate our commitment to them as future leaders of our race. I am pleased that Third World Press is publishing Useni's plays so that they can be more widely produced and seen.

Abena Joan P. Brown
President/Producer
ETA Creative Arts Foundation
Chicago, IL

# INTRODUCTION

*The Need to Develop Dramatic Material for Black Children*

If we are ever to have a children's theater which reflects the culture, heritage and history of the Black Experience, it is incumbent upon Black playwrights to develop dramatic material to support such an institution. Although all theater does not necessarily emanate from written material, a literature written expressly for theater provides it with a firmer foundation.

Judging by the paltry number of children's plays they have written, Black playwrights would lead us to believe Black children do not exist. While there has been an expansion in Black theater, the status of its children's theater leaves much to be desired. And because of this seeming apathy, Black children are compelled to watch plays that have little significance to their experience. As a result, Black children continue to be duped by *Peter Pan*, *Cinderella*, *Rumplestiltskin* and the perennial favorite, *Snow White and the Seven Dwarfs*. And when Black children are not watching these fantasies of white culture, they must endure adaptations of these same plays performed by Black people. The current trend of adapting children's stories originally written by white authors should be viewed with skepticism. Dramatic material that alleges to depict the Black Experience should be derived from Black culture and not be an imitiation of white culture.

Some of these adaptations may be appealing to Black children, but they can never capture the verve and ethos of the Black Experience. This can only be achieved when Black playwrights develop dramatic material that reflects our own history and culture. Of course it is easier for a Black playwright to write an adaptation from a story taken from Western literature and embellish it with Black dialect, dance and music. But this type of writing is simply a restatement of the coon show, minstrel, etc., which stigmatized early Black theater in this country.

It is time for Black playwrights to eradicate such stigmas and use their energies and creative talents to write authentic, dramatic material for Black children. There exists a reservoir of oral history, myths, folklore and Afrikan traditions that could serve as resources for Black playwrights. In addition, these materials would help enrich the development of Black children who need to be exposed to images they can identify with. The images being marketed by the various media produce few models that are positive and inspirational.

Image making should be foremost in the minds of Black playwrights when writing dramatic material for Black children. From images children get models, and from models, they get direction. We must *no* longer rely on models created by the white media to give direction to our children. Although the theater may not be the panacea for the problem, it can be a positive means to correct many of the distortions manufactured by the media. If theater is to have any real significance for Black children it must provide them with a greater awareness of their history and a greater appreciation of their culture.

This is not to say theater must always politicize (although political awareness should have high priority), but it should attempt to contribute to the positive development of Black children. This is indeed possible because good theater can be informative and still retain its artistic integrity. Black children need a theater that can raise their consciousness and challenge their intellect. They need a theater that embraces an Afrocentric view of the world so they have a frame of reference that is supportive of our struggle. They need a theater whose values are shaped by a collective need which benefits all Black people. The real theater is not a staged production but an enactment of our lives. Unless Black children learn how to cope with this stage, they will continue to act out roles that are inimical to our survival.

Black playwrights can make a significant contribution to Black theater if they develop more dramatic material for Black children. The images children associate with during their formative years will have a great impact on their adult lives. The challenge we Black people face is, Who will create these images? At present, the white dominated media, i.e., television, movies and theater, have a large edge. But that is simply because few Black playwrights have created images to counteract this advantage. Until we provide Black children with images created from an Afrocentric view of the universe, they will continue to be influenced by Western models.

There is an ancient Afrikan proverb that says "Children are the reward of life." We need dramatic material for Black children that supports this wisdom.

A Luta Continua
Useni Eugene Perkins

# BLACK FAIRY

## and other plays for children

# BLACK FAIRY

# Black Fairy

## A MUSICAL DRAMA FOR CHILDREN IN THREE ACTS

### USENI EUGENE PERKINS

### MUSIC BY ANTHONY LLORENS AND JAMI AYINDE

"Black Fairy" was first produced at the LaMont Zeno Theater, Better Boys Foundation Family Center, in April 1975 and was directed by Pemon Rami. Permission for the performance of this play must be obtained from ETA Creative Arts Foundation, Inc., 7558 S. South

# CHARACTERS

### (In Order of Appearance)

JOHNNY
BLACK FAIRY
WHITE FAIRY
SECOND WHITE FAIRY
BLACK BIRD
QUEEN MOTHER
AESOP
KING CROESUS
THE CROW
THE FOX
FIRST AFRICAN BOY
SECOND AFRICAN BOY
AFRICAN GIRL
ELDER
EGYPTIAN DANCER (MALE)
EGYPTIAN DANCER
  (FEMALE)
MR. SUN
MR. WATER
MR. MOON
FIRST SLAVE BOY
SECOND SLAVE BOY
SLAVE GIRL
UNCLE JULIUS
BRER RABBIT
SIS COW
MONKEY
LION
ELEPHANT
STAGOLEE
FIRST GHETCOLONY BOY

SECOND GHETCOLONY
BOY
LEADBELLY
DRUMMER
EXTRAS

# SONGS

*We Are the White Fairies*

*If Only I Had Some Magic*

*Tell Them They Are Beautiful*

*Black Land of the Nile*

*Langa More (More Sun)*

*Afrikan Children*

*Streets of Harlem*

*Bad Stagolee*

*Black Men Can Be Beautiful*

*Little Sally Walker*

*Chula Lu*

*Shoo Fly, Don't Bother Me*

*Black Fairy*

*Skip to My Lou*

*Tell Them They Are Beautiful*

*Hey, Black Child*

## PROLOGUE

BEDROOM IN HARLEM TENEMENT


## ACT I

SCENE ONE:          GARDEN IN FAIRYLAND

SCENE TWO:          HOME  OF QUEEN MOTHER

SCENE THREE:        THE COURT OF KING CROESUS

SCENE FOUR:         THE BANK OF THE NILE RIVER IN EGYPT


## ACT II

SCENE ONE:          A VILLAGE IN EAST AFRIKA

SCENE TWO:          A SOUTHERN PLANTATION


## ACT III

SCENE ONE:          A STREET IN HARLEM


## EPILOGUE

BEDROOM IN HARLEM TENEMENT

---

# PROLOGUE
## BEDROOM IN HARLEM TENEMENT

*(It is late night and a small boy is lying on a cot. He begins to cry and moves around restlessly, as though he is unable to sleep. A bright light flashes in the room and Black Fairy appears. She wears a dirty dress and her wings are tarnished. Upon seeing her, the little boy jumps up in a frightened manner.)*

### BLACK FAIRY
*(trying to calm the boy's fear)* Don't be afraid, little boy. I will not harm you. I come as a friend.

### JOHNNY
*(still frightened)* But who...are you? Where did you come from?

### BLACK FAIRY
*(comforting)* I'm the Black Fairy, and I come from Fairyland. What is your name, little boy?

### JOHNNY
*(feels somewhat relieved)* Johnny. But you don't look like a fairy to me. And if you are...I don't believe in them anyway.

### BLACK FAIRY
What do you believe in, Johnny?

### JOHNNY
Nuthin'. I don't believe in nuthin'.

### BLACK FAIRY
Is that why you were crying?

### JOHNNY
Ain't none of your business.

---

**BLACK FAIRY**

But I would like to help you if I can.

**JOHNNY**

Can't nobody help me.

**BLACK FAIRY**

How do you know...if you won't let me try?

**JOHNNY**

Nobody cares about Black people. If they did...my family wouldn't be on welfare, and I would have a new bike and some nice clothes, and we wouldn't have to eat beans and cornbread everyday.

**BLACK FAIRY**

So that's why you're crying. You would like to have things better.

**JOHNNY**

Being poor ain't nothin' to be proud of.

**BLACK FAIRY**

That's true. But you don't have to be ashamed 'cause you're poor.

**JOHNNY**

And Black people don't have nothing!

**BLACK FAIRY**

That's not true.

**JOHNNY**

Well, you so smart...then show me!

**BLACK FAIRY**

*(tries to find the correct words)* Well...er...well...there is...er...

---

**JOHNNY**

You see...you can't think of anything. And you're supposed to be a fairy. Can't your magic help you think of something?

**BLACK FAIRY**

I...er...don't have any magic.

**JOHNNY**

The white fairies have magic. That's why white people have every-thing.

**BLACK FAIRY**

But there are other things besides magic.

**JOHNNY**

You're just like all the rest. Nuthin' but talk. Why don't you go away. I don't need you anyhow. *(begins to cry again)*

**BLACK FAIRY**

But won't you let me try to make you happy?

**JOHNNY**

No...go away! You can't make me happy. You're Black just like me. Go away...go away! *(Black Fairy looks sad and slowly withdraws and disappears as the bright light flashes again.)*

## ACT ONE: SCENE ONE
## A GARDEN IN FAIRYLAND

*(All the fairies are white except, of course, Black Fairy. The white fairies are dressed in pretty white dresses with silver wings. Black Fairy sits alone as the other fairies dance in a circle and sing the following song:)*

## <u>WE ARE THE WHITE FAIRIES</u>

We are the white fairies
The most beautiful fairies in the world
We are the white fairies
As precious as the whitest of pearls

We make all of our children happy
And give them whatever they need
For we are the white fairies
And all we do are good deeds

We turn pumpkins into carriages
We turn paupers into kings
We turn rags into riches
We turn damsels into queens

We turn slums into castles
We turn night into day
We turn ugliness into beauty
We turn grass into hay

We make all of our children happy
And give them whatever they need
For we are the white fairies
And all we do are good deeds

---

We turn villains into heroes
We turn bad into good
We turn futility into hope
We make diamonds from wood

We do everything that's right
Because we are white.

*(They dance around Black Fairy and make fun of her. Finally, all but two of the white fairies leave. The fairies who remain begin to whisper to each other.)*

### FIRST WHITE FAIRY

Poor ugly thing. She's got no one to talk to.

### SECOND WHITE FAIRY

Yes, isn't it a pity? *(Black Fairy holds her head down.)*

### FIRST WHITE FAIRY

And look at that dirty dress and those wings. Why, she looks terrible.

### SECOND WHITE FAIRY

How did she get here looking like that? She's so dirty and black.

### FIRST WHITE FAIRY

Well, can't you say something? *(Black Fairy remains silent.)*

### SECOND WHITE FAIRY

Maybe she's from another planet.

### FIRST WHITE FAIRY

*(shakes Black Fairy)* Now see here...whoever you are. Don't you realize that you should speak when someone asks you a question? How do you expect to be a fairy if you are so spiteful? Fairies are supposed to be happy.

**SECOND WHITE FAIRY**

Maybe she's not a real fairy.

**BLACK FAIRY**

*(looks up)* I'm a Black fairy.

**FIRST WHITE FAIRY**

You mean Black people have fairies?

**SECOND WHITE FAIRY**

What's this universe coming to?

**FIRST WHITE FAIRY**

No wonder she's so dirty.

**SECOND WHITE FAIRY**

Of course. How could she expect to be anything else?

**FIRST WHITE FAIRY**

But why was she made into a fairy? She's not like the rest of us.
*(looks Black Fairy over)*

**SECOND WHITE FAIRY**

Yes, and how can she make Black children happy when she's so sad
herself?

**FIRST WHITE FAIRY**

Perhaps she has special magic. *(withdraws a few steps)*

**SECOND WHITE FAIRY**

You think so? I thought all fairies had the same magic. *(withdraws
also)*

**FIRST WHITE FAIRY**

Since she looks so different, maybe she does have different magic.

---

## SECOND WHITE FAIRY

*(cautiously)* Black Fairy, is your magic different from ours?

## BLACK FAIRY

*(begins to weep)* I've no magic.

## SECOND WHITE FAIRY

No magic! Why, I never heard of a fairy who had no magic. How can you make Black children happy without magic?

## FIRST WHITE FAIRY

*(begins laughing)* She has no magic. And yet she calls herself a fairy. Stupid little thing. *(Second White Fairy laughs also)* Come, we have no time to spend with such trash. Imagine, no magic. *(They continue laughing as they walk away.)*

## BLACK FAIRY

*(sobbing)* Oh, if I could only become a real fairy and have some magic. I'll never be able to make my children happy this way. *(begins singing in a melancholy voice)*

## IF ONLY I HAD SOME MAGIC

Please give me some magic
Please give me some magic
Please give me some magic
So I can make every Black child free

If only I had some magic
I would make every boy a king
If only I had some magic
I would make every girl a queen

I would make it a better world
For everyone to enjoy

I would make it a better world
For every girl and boy

If only I had some magic
There would be no more wars
I would bring peace to everyone
And there would be no more quarrels

*(During the song Black Bird appears, but Black Fairy doesn't notice her until she has finished singing.)*

### BLACK BIRD

Why are you sad?

### BLACK FAIRY

Because I have no magic to make my children happy.

### BLACK BIRD

You're a fairy aren't you?

### BLACK FAIRY

Yes, but I'm a Black fairy.

### BLACK BIRD

Is that anything to be ashamed of?

### BLACK FAIRY

All the white fairies have magic. How can I make our Black children happy without any magic?

### BLACK BIRD

It depends on what you tell them. Magic is only make-believe, and our children do not need to grow up in a make-believe world. You need to tell them the truth and try to help make them feel proud of who they are. The magic of truth is much more powerful than the magic of make-believe.

---

**BLACK FAIRY**

But how can I make them feel proud when they have so very little?

**BLACK BIRD**

This is true. But if you help them to appreciate what little they do have, then you will be making an important first step.

**BLACK FAIRY**

But what can I tell them?

**BLACK BIRD**

Tell them that they're beautiful. Tell them that they're Black. *(begins singing)*

<u>**TELL THEM THEY ARE BEAUTIFUL**</u>

> **Tell them they are beautiful**
> **As beautiful as the stars**
> **Tell them they are beautiful**
> **As wonderful as their hearts**

> **O tell them, O tell them**
> **That being Black is nothing to be ashamed of**
> **O tell them, O tell them**
> **That being Black is something to be proud of**

> **Tell them they are beautiful**
> **As beautiful as the trees**
> **Tell them they are tender**
> **As tender as a breeze**

> **O tell them, O tell them**
> **That being Black is nothing to be ashamed of**
> **O tell them, O tell them**
> **That being Black is something to be proud of**

**BLACK FAIRY**

*(after the song has been completed)* That was so beautiful. But it's easy for them to believe you. You're a Black Bird, and your voice sounds like a symphony of violins.

**BLACK BIRD**

But they will believe you too if only you believe in yourself. First you must feel a sense of pride before you can transmit it to others.

**BLACK FAIRY**

Oh, I would do anything to make my children happy. Please, Black Bird, is there anything you can do to help me!

**BLACK BIRD**

Maybe there is. I believe what you say. Come grab hold of my wing, and I will take you to someone who can give you something even better than magic. *(Takes hold of Black Fairy's hand. A cloud of black smoke appears as the scene ends.)*


## ACT ONE: SCENE TWO
## A ROOM IN QUEEN MOTHER'S HOUSE

*(Black Fairy and Black Bird appear in Queen Mother's house. Queen Mother is dressed in a beautiful black gown and is watering her plants.)*

**BLACK FAIRY**

*(awed)* Who is she?

**BLACK BIRD**

Queen Mother, the daughter of Afrika.

**BLACK FAIRY**

She's so beautiful!

---

**BLACK BIRD**

She's more than that. Come and you will see. *(takes Black Fairy to Queen Mother)*

**QUEEN MOTHER**

Well, if it's not my dear friend, Black Bird. I've not seen you in some time. And who is this charming lady with you? *(stops her watering)*

**BLACK BIRD**

This is Black Fairy, Queen Mother. I met her this morning.

**QUEEN MOTHER**

I've never met a fairy before. Come, dear, don't be afraid. *(beckons Black Fairy to come closer)*

**BLACK FAIRY**

*(in front of Queen Mother)* Thank you, Queen Mother. It is indeed an honor for me to be in the presence of so gracious a lady.

**QUEEN MOTHER**

*(flattered)* You need not be so kind, my dear. I'm only mortal.

**BLACK BIRD**

But your spirit is immortal.

**QUEEN MOTHER**

Only because Afrika still lives. Now, what have I done to deserve such a visit?

**BLACK BIRD**

We thought you may be able to help us, Queen Mother.

**QUEEN MOTHER**

Me help a fairy? What about her magic?

### BLACK FAIRY

I have no magic.

### BLACK BIRD

The Black Fairy is unhappy because she feels she has nothing to offer our Black children.

### QUEEN MOTHER

Ridiculous. Of course she has something to offer Black children.

### BLACK FAIRY

But when I go to their homes, Queen Mother, I only see human misery.

### QUEEN MOTHER

Of course, many of our children live under poor conditions, but that doesn't mean they're in complete misery. Can't you see the beauty that's in their tender eyes or feel the warmth that's in their hearts?

### BLACK FAIRY

I can only see misery which I cannot change. And there is no beauty in that.

### QUEEN MOTHER

What you lack, my dear, is a real appreciation of the beauty of Black people. I'm sure that if you had a better appreciation of your heritage, you would not feel as you do. Perhaps we can do something about that. Black Bird, do you think you could take us through the past so that we might show Black Fairy something about our people that would make her feel proud?

### BLACK BIRD

I think that can be arranged. *(takes the hand of Queen Mother and Black Fairy)* Now just hold tight and your request will be my command. *(A cloud of smoke appears as the lights go out, indicating a journey back through history.)*

## ACT ONE: SCENE THREE
## THE COURT OF KING CROESUS IN LYDIA, GREECE

*(When they arrive at the court, King Croesus is seen seated on his throne, and Aesop stands facing him. Queen Mother, Black Bird and Black Fairy remain in the background.)*

### BLACK FAIRY
Such a lovely place. Where are we?

### QUEEN MOTHER
We are in the court of King Croesus of Greece around the year 620 A.D.

### BLACK FAIRY
*(points to the King)* And is that King Croesus seated on the throne?

### QUEEN MOTHER
Yes, it is.

### BLACK FAIRY
And who is the Black man he is talking to?

### BLACK BIRD
That's Aesop. He's the King's personal confidant and ambassador.

### BLACK FAIRY
*(surprised)* Why, I thought Aesop was white.

### QUEEN MOTHER
That's only because the white historians tried to conceal who he actually was. They refused to admit that some of the world's greatest thinkers were Black people. Aesop was one of the greatest thinkers the world has seen. Yet, his name is not mentioned in the same breath with Plato or Socrates, both of whom owe much of their wisdom to Aesop. Why don't we move a little closer and hear what they are saying. *(They move closer to King Croesus and Aesop.)*

**AESOP**

My dear king, I've been throughout Greece and found that there is much division between the states.

**KING CROESUS**

As I expected, Aesop. But now that you have been made my ambassador, I'm sure we can look forward to better times.

**AESOP**

I truly hope so, your majesty.

**KING CROESUS**

Why, with your wisdom and wit, I know we can convince all the heads of states how important it is for Greece to remain a united country. There are many enemies who would like to destroy us and, therefore, it's imperative that we have unity. Greece will be forever indebted to you, Aesop.

**AESOP**

I'm always willing to serve in the interest of my country, your majesty.

**KING CROESUS**

Won't you tell me one of your fables, Aesop? I always enjoy hearing them so very much.

**AESOP**

As you request, your majesty. I don't believe I've told you the story of the Fox and the Grapes. *(The following fable can be simply acted out during Aesop's recitation without changing the scene. A child can be dressed like a fox and a prop can hold a bunch of grapes.)*

# THE FOX AND THE GRAPES

Mister Fox was just about famished, and thirsty too, when he stole into a vineyard where sunripened grapes were hanging up on a trellis in a tempting show, but too high for him to reach. He took a run and a jump, snapping at the nearest bunch, but missed. Again and again he jumped, only to miss the luscious prize. At last, worn out with his efforts, he retreated, muttering: "Well, I never really wanted those grapes anyway, I am sure they are sour, and perhaps wormy in the bargain."

### KING CROESUS
You are so right, Aesop. Any fool can despise what he cannot get.

### QUEEN MOTHER
*(in background)* Today we call that SOUR GRAPES.

### KING CROESUS
Thank you, Aesop. You always make my day much brighter and wiser. Now I must tend to some other business. Please report to me immediately after you come back from Athens. *(alights from throne and departs)*

### QUEEN MOTHER
Now maybe we can talk to Aesop. *(Queen Mother, Black Bird and Black Fairy approach Aesop.)*

### QUEEN MOTHER
King Croesus is correct. Your fables do make the day brighter.

### AESOP
*(turns in surprise)* Why, if it isn't Queen Mother. And as beautiful as ever.

**QUEEN MOTHER**

Your words are always gracious, Aesop. May I introduce you to Black Fairy? I think you have already met Black Bird.

**AESOP**

*(extends greetings)* I've always wanted to meet a real fairy.

**BLACK FAIRY**

But I'm not a real fairy.

**AESOP**

Then why do you have wings?

**BLACK BIRD**

Black Fairy doesn't have magic like the other fairies. That's why she feels the way she does.

**AESOP**

That's too bad. And she's so pretty.

**QUEEN MOTHER**

But she doesn't realize her own beauty, Aesop. So we are taking her through the past...so that she can begin to see the real beauty of Black people.

**BLACK FAIRY**

I'm beginning to see it already. *(to Aesop)* I think that your telling stories through animals is fascinating. Animals have a special appeal to children.

**AESOP**

That's right, Black Fairy. You see, animals are creatures of God too and have many of the same feelings as do humans. Animal stories are almost as old as man himself, especially among my brothers in Afrika and India, they are quite popular.

---

**BLACK BIRD**

However, in our society, Aesop, animal stories are used to express violence and the ridiculous. We call them cartoons.

**AESOP**

That is indeed unfortunate. I only tell animal stories which have a moral to them. For it is man's lack of morality that makes him so thoughtless and cruel.

**QUEEN MOTHER**

Before we go, Aesop, perhaps you can give Black Fairy some advice with one of your fables.

**AESOP**

*(thinking)* Well let me see. Yes, I know a fable that just might be appropriate. It's called "The Crow and the Pitcher." *(Again, the fable can be acted out during Aesop's recitation.)*

## THE CROW AND THE PITCHER

A crow, so thirsty that he could not even caw, came upon a pitcher which once had been full of water, but when he put his beak into the pitcher's mouth, he found that only a little water was left in it. Strain and strive as he might he was not able to reach far enough down to get at it. He tried to break the pitcher, then to overturn it, but his strength was not equal to the task.

Just as he was about to give up in despair a thought came to him. He picked up a pebble and dropped it into the pitcher. Then he took another pebble and dropped that into the pitcher. One by one he kept dropping pebbles into the pitcher until the water mounted to the brim. He drank and drank until his thirst was quenched.

## BLACK FAIRY

*(scratching head)* Forgive me, Aesop, but I don't quite understand the logic of your fable.

## QUEEN MOTHER

Don't worry, my dear. You will someday. I think that the message you gave her, Aesop, will become clear to her, and when it does, I'm sure she'll begin to see things differently.

## BLACK BIRD

*(scratches head too)* I must admit, Aesop, you have stunted me too this time.

## AESOP

I will be happy to explain my logic.

## QUEEN MOTHER

No, Aesop, I think it's better if they found out for themselves. Come, my children, we must be leaving.

## BLACK FAIRY

Thank you so much, Aesop. *(kisses him on the forehead)*

## BLACK BIRD

That goes for me too. *(kisses him also)* Where to now, Queen Mother?

## QUEEN MOTHER

You'll see. Goodbye, Aesop. *(Again a cloud of smoke appears, signifying a change in time and space.)*

---

# ACT ONE: SCENE FOUR
## THE BANK OF THE NILE
## RIVER IN ANCIENT EGYPT

*(Queen Mother, Black Bird and Black Fairy appear in the background. A young boy and girl are kneeling in prayer near the water, facing the sun. Beside them is a dead cat wrapped in a red cloth. When they finish praying they begin to do a ritualistic-styled dance which can be accompanied by a flute or violin. They complete their dance and then place the cat in a small tomb with other items. They then kneel and pray again. Finally they leave.)*

### BLACK FAIRY
*(holding back tears)* Makes me almost want to cry.

### BLACK BIRD
It was a touching scene.

### QUEEN MOTHER
*(looks at tomb)* The Egyptians buried many of their animals in this manner. The cat was very sacred to them. In fact, anyone caught killing a cat was often put to death. And the head of the cat can be found on many Egyptian deities.

### BLACK BIRD
What about black birds, Queen Mother? Are they sacred too?

### QUEEN MOTHER
*(smiles)* Do not worry, Black Bird. You'll be with us for a long time.

### BLACK FAIRY
To whom were they praying, Queen Mother?

### QUEEN MOTHER
To their sun god, RA. The ancient Egyptians were a very religious people. They had deities for just about everything.

## BLACK FAIRY

And they were Black too!

## QUEEN MOTHER

Of course they were, my dear. We are in Afrika, the mother country of Black people.

## BLACK FAIRY

I never thought of Egypt as being part of Afrika.

## QUEEN MOTHER

That is only because most white historians make it appear that Egypt is separate from Africa. *(begins singing)*

## BLACK LAND OF THE NILE

**There once was a land**
**That stood along the Nile**
**She was located in a valley**
**That stretched for many miles**

**The sun always shone upon her face**
**She was the cradle of civilization**
**And other people envied her**
**From far away nations**

**O Egypt, O Egypt**
**Black Land of the Nile**

**Afrikans came to Egypt**
**From the country of Sudan**
**And crossed the Sahara desert**
**In colorful caravans**

**They came from Ethiopia**
**And Mali and Timbuktu**
**They traveled from ancient Ghana**

And also Cameroon
O Egypt, O Egypt
Black Land of the Nile

Egypt was a mighty nation
They built pyramids in the sand
And they even stand today
As one of the greatest feats of man

Egypt had many cities
Which lasted for thousands of years
Her people worked very hard
Despite their sweat and tears

O Egypt, O Egypt
Black Land of the Nile

Egypt is Afrika
And the sun still shines on her
But Egypt is Afrika
And the sun still shines on her

O Egypt, O Egypt
Black Land of the Nile


**BLACK FAIRY**

*(sighs)* I feel like I could stay here forever.


**BLACK BIRD**

That's impossible. There are many children in the Black community who need you. I'm sure that you are being missed right this minute.

**BLACK FAIRY**

Yes, I suppose you're right. But how can I help them without any magic?

**QUEEN MOTHER**

I doubt if even magic can cure their ills. There is still much that you must learn. Come let us go. *(The three again join hands, and a cloud of smoke appears as the lights go out.)*

## ACT TWO: SCENE ONE
## A VILLAGE IN EAST AFRIKA

*(Three small children are gathered on the ground around a village Elder. Queen Mother, Black Bird and Black Fairy appear in the background.)*

### BLACK FAIRY
Where are we now, Queen Mother?

### QUEEN MOTHER
Near Kenya, on the East Coast of Afrika.

### BLACK FAIRY
Why, the children look just like the children who live in America.

### BLACK BIRD
Of course they do. They are all brothers and sisters...aren't they?

### BLACK FAIRY
I never thought of it like that, Black Bird.

### QUEEN MOTHER
It's time that you did, dear, for all Black children in America are descendants of Afrika.

### BLACK BIRD
And many of their ancestors lived in East Afrika. Isn't that right, Queen Mother?

### QUEEN MOTHER
Yes, but Blacks were taken from other parts of Africa as well. West Africa, Central Africa and even Azania or South Africa, as it is commonly called.

**BLACK FAIRY**

The children seem so happy. I wonder what they're doing?

**QUEEN MOTHER**

I think they are listening to a story by one of the village Elders.

**BLACK BIRD**

Perhaps we can listen too.

**QUEEN MOTHER**

That's a good idea. Let's do it. *(They walk over to the children and the Elder. The Elder is seated on a wooden stool. The children are very attentive.)*

**ELDER**

*(to children)* Have you ever thought about why the Moon and Sun live in the sky?

**FIRST BOY**

No, not I.

**SECOND BOY**

Me neither.

**GIRL**

I suppose so that they can bring light to the earth.

**ELDER**

Well, if you'll be nice children, I'll tell you why. *(The children nod their approval.)* Well once upon a time, over thousands of years ago, the Sun and the Moon used to live on earth. Now one of their best friends was Mr. Water. However, Mr. Sun would always visit Mr. Water, but Mr. Water would never return the visit. Mr. Sun became concerned about this and one day decided to ask Mr. Water why he never visited him and Mrs. Moon. *(Mr. Sun and Mr. Water appear on stage as he narrates the story.)*

MR. SUN: Mr. Water, I've been concerned about why you've never paid my home a visit. I visit your home many times.

MR. WATER: It's nothing personal, Mr. Sun. You and I have always been the best of friends. However, I've not come to your house because I didn't think it was large enough to accommodate me and my friends. As you know, wherever I go, my friends must come along too.

MR. SUN: Oh, if that's the only reason you haven't visited us then you have nothing to worry about. There's plenty of room in our house.

MR. WATER: Well, if that's the case, then I'll be over to visit you the first thing tomorrow.

MR. SUN: Fine. We'll be expecting you tomorrow. This will make Mrs. Moon quite happy. *(They both exit.)*

### ELDER

So, on the following morning at the home of Mr. Sun and Mrs. Moon, Mr. Sun was very anxious, anticipating the visit of Mr. Water. *(the home of Mr. Sun and Mrs. Moon the next day)*

MR. SUN: This will be a great day for us.

MRS. MOON: And just why is that, dear?

MR. SUN: Because Mr. Water is going to visit us.

MRS. MOON: That's wonderful. I'll be sure to clean the house well and prepare a good dinner.

MR. SUN: I thought that would make you happy.

**MRS. MOON**: Of course. I think that Mr. Water is a marvelous person and have always looked forward to him visiting our home. *(They fade out.)*

### ELDER

So on that very evening, Mr. Sun and Mrs. Moon waited patiently for Mr. Water to visit them. Mrs. Moon had prepared a delicious dinner and everything was in order for Mr. Water. *(same day, that evening)*

**MRS. MOON**: Someone is at the door, dear. Would you answer it?

**MR. SUN**: It's probably Mr. Water and his friends. *(goes to door and greets Mr. Water)* Good evening, Mr. Water. It's so nice of you to pay Mrs. Moon and me a visit.

**MR. WATER**: Thank you, Mr. Sun. I've been looking forward to this visit for a long time. May we come in now?

**MR. SUN**: Of course, please do. *(beckons to Mr. Water to come in)*

### ELDER

So, as Mr. Water entered the house of Mr. Sun and Mrs. Moon, he began to motion to his friends to follow. And follow they did. All kinds of fishes and sea animals began to fill up the room.

**MR. WATER**: Can more of my friends come in?

**MR. SUN**: Of course, Mr. Water. We have plenty room.

### ELDER

So, Mr. Water continued to motion his friends to come in and the room continued to fill up. But Mr. Sun and Mrs. Moon, despite the fact that the water had risen up to their waists, refused to concede that they were running out of room.

**MR. WATER:** Your room is filling up pretty rapidly. Do you still want us to come in?

**MR. SUN:** *(water at his shoulders now)* Yes...yes. We still have room.

**MRS. MOON:** Since we invited you to our house, we will welcome all of your friends.

**MR. WATER:** Alright, but I'm warning you, I'll be over your heads in a few moments.

### ELDER

But again, Mr. Sun and Mrs. Moon continued to ignore the warnings of Mr. Water, and so by this time the water had completely filled their house, and they were forced to go onto the roof. But the water very soon overflowed on the roof, and Mr. Sun and Mrs. Moon were forced to go up into the sky, where they have remained ever since. *(Mr. Sun and Mrs. Moon fade out.)*

### BLACK FAIRY

It's an amusing story, even if it is unbelievable.

### QUEEN MOTHER

But you must remember that many Afrikans do not make a distinction between animate and inanimate things. Therefore, to them, it was quite conceivable that the sun and moon could've lived on earth at one time and possessed human qualities.

### BLACK BIRD

Yes, and anyway it's just a myth, perhaps no more ridiculous than *Jack and the Beanstalk*, *Snow White and the Seven Dwarfs* or even *Humpty Dumpty*. All people have a way of expressing their particular culture. The story about the sun and the moon merely represents the folklore of these Afrikan people. If we were to go to Ghana, Dahomey, Uganda or Senegal, you would probably hear different versions of this same story.

## QUEEN MOTHER

Very well put, Black Bird.

## BLACK BIRD

*(points to young man and woman)* Look, Queen Mother, they are beginning to dance. *(The children begin to dance to the beat of a drummer. The dance should be done to the tune of "Langa More" or another Afrikan song.)*

## LANGA MORE  (More Sun)

Tap, tap, oh, more sun
Tap, tap, oh, more sun, hey, hey, hey
You are teaching us, come in and see
The feast of the feet, hey, hey, hey
It makes us move, come in and see
The feast of the feet. We are walking, muh!
We are gathering, we shall pat each other, oh!
We are going to be mad
We are walking, hum, we are gathering
We shall pat each other, oh!
We are going to be mad
We are going to hit the sun

We are going to hit the sun more, hey, hey, hey, hey
You are teaching us, come in see
The feast of the feet, hey, hey, hey, hey
It causes us to move.
Come in and see the feast of the feet
We are going to hit the sun more
We are going to hit the sun, hum, hum

## BLACK FAIRY

Such a beautiful song. And the dancing was just wonderful, too.

---

## QUEEN MOTHER

Afrikans love to sing and dance. Their songs and dances all have meaning and are actually a part of their total culture.

## BLACK FAIRY

And just think, many of the children in our community have no knowledge of this.

## BLACK BIRD

True. But that is where you can begin to help them.

## BLACK FAIRY

How will telling them about their culture help to save them from poverty?

## QUEEN MOTHER

You have a good point. However, I think we will be better able to answer this question when we have completed our trip.

## BLACK FAIRY

There's still more to see?

## QUEEN MOTHER

Of course. We must now begin to see what part of our Afrikan heritage still exists in America. Yes, we are going back to where we started, although the real roots of our culture are right here on Afrikan soil.

## BLACK FAIRY

I hate to leave.

## QUEEN MOTHER

I'm sure you'll return someday. *(to Black Bird)* Are your wings strong enough to take us on another flight, Black Bird?

**BLACK BIRD**

*(smiles)* Yes, as strong as Afrika herself.


**QUEEN MOTHER**

*(returns smile)* Then we should have no trouble getting to our next destination. *(Cloud of black smoke appears as the scene closes out.)*


## ACT TWO: SCENE TWO
## A SOUTHERN PLANTATION AROUND 1705

*(As the scene opens, children are running around. Uncle Julius is seated on a log near a wooden fence. He is twiddling on a piece of wood. "Go Down Moses" can be heard in the background. Queen Mother, Black Fairy and Black Bird appear and remain in the background.)*


**BLACK FAIRY**

*(after looking around)* Why, we are on a slave plantation. How horrible!


**QUEEN MOTHER**

Horrible, yes. But it's a part of our history that we can never forget. American slavery attempted to destroy all of our Afrikan heritage. The slave masters realized that it was easier to oppress people when they had no heritage of their own to turn to. That's why they broke up the family and did not allow the slaves to speak their native language. But our people have always been strong. And it was impossible for them to take all of our heritage away from us. In fact, had we not retained some of our Afrikan heritage, I wonder where any of us would be today.


**BLACK BIRD**

That looks like Uncle Julius!

## BLACK FAIRY

Who is Uncle Julius?

## QUEEN MOTHER

Why, he's just an old man who tells stories to children to make them happy. Some of the young people today feel that Uncle Julius was an Uncle Tom. But that is because they do not understand that he only catered to white folks so he could do something for his own people. And white folks tried to create their own version of Uncle Julius in such plays as "Green Pastures." But Uncle Julius' stories were written by Charles W. Chesnutt, one of our first Black authors. And the children simply adored him.

## BLACK BIRD

See, he's talking to some now.

## BLACK FAIRY

Can we listen?

## QUEEN MOTHER

Of course we can. *(She leads Black Fairy and Black Bird to where Uncle Julius is talking to the children.)*

## FIRST BOY

Uncle Julius, won't cha tell us a story?

## SECOND BOY

Yeah...one of dem crazy tales.

## UNCLE JULIUS

*(smiles)* You mean Brer Rabbit?

## GIRL

Yeah, de funny rabbit.

## UNCLE JULIUS

Alright, children. Uncle Julius is always happy to tell his children a story, especially 'bout Brer Rabbit. Now, like always you have to sit real quiet and pay close attention. *(The children comply as Uncle Julius narrates the following tale. Like the other animal tales, this one can also be acted out as it is being told.)* Well, one hot summer day, Brer Rabbit was feelin' pretty thirsty, and as he was walking down de road, he spotted Sis Cow. Now, Sis Cow was standing under a persimmon tree and looking pretty upset. Of course she had a lot of milk stored in her bags, but Brer Rabbit knew better 'n to ask her for some, 'cause he and Sis Cow didn't git along too good. So Brer Rabbit began to think of some way to git some of Sis Cow's milk. So, he said:

**BRER RABBIT:** Good mornin', Sis Cow.

**SIS COW:** Good mornin', Brer Rabbit.

**BRER RABBIT:** What are you doin' standin' under de persimmon tree, Sis Cow?

**SIS COW:** I was afraid you'd ask something like dat.

**BRER RABBIT:** Well!

**SIS COW:** I'm waiting for some of dese persimmons to fall down. *(looks up)*

**BRER RABBIT:** But dey ain't ripe yet, Sis Cow. Don'cha know that they don't fall down til dey're ripe? You might be here all summer.

**SIS COW:** *(kicks tree)* And I wanted one so much.

**BRER RABBIT:** Wait, I got an idea! Why don't you go up on dat dere hill and git a good start and use your horns to knock some of dem down. I'm sure you git some dat way.

---

## UNCLE JULIUS

So Sis Cow took Brer Rabbit's advice and went to de top of de hill. She den lowered her head and came running down de hill till her horns went smack right into de tree. But she couldn't git 'em out.

> **SIS COW:** Brer Rabbit, won't you help me git my horns out of dis tree?

> **BRER RABBIT:** I'm pretty weak, Sis Cow. Ain't had nuthin' to drink all day. Perhaps if I had some of your milk...

> **SIS COW:** *(realizing she had been tricked)* Alright, Brer Rabbit. As usual you win. You can have as much of de milk you want. Just help me git my horns out of dis here tree.

## UNCLE JULIUS

So after Brer Rabbit had taken all the milk he could drink, he den tried to help Sis Cow git her horns out of de tree. But Brer Rabbit had drunk so much milk, he was too tired to be of any help. So he just laid down next to Sis Cow and went to sleep.

## FIRST BOY

Dat Brer Rabbit sure is tricky.

## SECOND BOY

Yeah, he sure is. But he ain't as tricky as Brer Fox, is he Uncle Julius?

## UNCLE JULIUS

Well, I really don' know. Both of 'em are pretty smart.

## GIRL

I like Brer Rabbit de best. He's cuter too.

**UNCLE JULIUS**

Now maybe you children will recite me some of those animal rhymes I done taught ya.

**FIRST BOY**

Ok, I'm first.

**GIRL**

Where's ya manners? Don'cha know ladies first?

**SECOND BOY**

Who said you was a lady?

**GIRL**

*(balls up her fist)* I said so. Wanna make somethin' of it?

**UNCLE JULIUS**

Now...now, children. Dat's no way to act. Ladies go first. Dat's somethin' we men folks must do...whether we likes it or not.

**FIRST BOY**

*(pouting)* Alright...let her go 'head.

**GIRL**

**THE ROOSTER AND THE CHICKEN**

**De rooster and de chicken had a fight,**
**De chicken knocked de rooster out of sight,**
**De rooster told de chicken, dat's alright.**

**SECOND BOY**

Dat's pretty good, even for a girl. But how 'bout dis one?

## BEDBUG

De June-bug's got de golden wing
De lightning-bug de flame
De bedbug's got no wing at all
But he gets dere just de same

De pumpkin bug's got a pumpkin smell
De squash-bug smells de worst
But de perfume of dat old bedbug
It's enough to make you burst

When dat bedbug comes down to my house
I take my walking cane
Go get a pot and scald him hot
Good-bye, Miss Liza Jane


### UNCLE JULIUS
*(turns to First Boy)* Now it's ya turn.

### FIRST BOY

## RABBIT SOUP

Rabbit soup! Rabbit Soup!
Rabbit et my turnip top!
Rabbit hop, rabbit jump,
Rabbit hide behind that stump.
Rabbit stop, twelve o'clock.
Killed dat rabbit with a rock.
Rabbit's mine. Rabbit's skint.
Clean him off and take him in.
Rabbit's on. Dance and whoop!
We gonna have some rabbit soup.

## GIRL

It's your turn now, Uncle Julius.

## UNCLE JULIUS

But I done told mines already.

## SECOND BOY

But you didn't tell us a rhyme.

## FIRST BOY

Dat's right, Uncle Julius.

## UNCLE JULIUS

Lardy me. You children sure 'nough know how to gang up on a guy. OK...I'll tell you de one 'bout de signifying monkey. *(This part can either be staged or read, depending on resources, facilities and performers.)*

## SIGNIFYING MONKEY*

NARRATOR: Said the Signifying Monkey to the Lion one day:

MONKEY: Hey, there's a big elephant down the way. He's goin' round talking, I'm sorry to say, 'bout your mama in a scandalous way. He's talkin' 'bout your mama and your grandma too! And he don't show too much respect for you. Now you weren't here and I sure am glad, 'cause what he said 'bout your ma made me mad.

CHORUS: The Lion said:

LION: Yeah, well I'll fix him. I'll tear that elephant limb from limb.

---

*written by Oscar Brown, Jr.

---

**NARRATOR:** Then he shook the jungle with a mighty roar. Took off like a shot from a forty-four. He found the elephant in the tall grass and said:

**LION:** I come to punch you in your long nose.

**NARRATOR:** The elephant looked at the lion in surprise and said:

**ELEPHANT:** Boy, you better go pick on somebody your size.

**NARRATOR:** The Lion wouldn't listen, he made a pass. The elephant slapped him down in the grass. The Lion roared and sprang from the ground, and that's when the elephant really went to town. I mean he whipped that Lion for the rest of the day, and still I don't see how the Lion got away. But he dragged on off more dead than alive, and that's when that monkey started his signifyin' jive.

**CHORUS:** Signifying Monkey, stay up in your tree. You are always lyin' and signifyin', but you better not monkey with me.

**NARRATOR:** The monkey looked down and said:

**MONKEY:** Owwee! What is this beat up mess I see! Is that you, Lion, ha ha, do tell. He whipped your head to a fare-de-well. Give you a beating that was rough enough, and you suppose to be King of the Jungle? Ain't that some stuff. Why, you overgrown pussycat, don't you roar, or I'll hop down there and whip you some more.

*(After the Signifying Monkey is over, Uncle Julius stands and faces the audience.)*

## UNCLE JULIUS

Ok – now let's all do one together! *(raises his hands and motions to the audience to join him)* After I sing a line – you nice folks say, "Yes, sir!" Alright, I want everybody to join in. Let's go! *(begins singing)*

## DID YOU FEED MY COW

Did you feed my cow?
*Yes, sir!*
Will you tell me how?
*Yes, sir!*
Oh, what did you give her?
*Corn and hay.*
Oh, what did you give her?
*Corn and hay.*
Did you milk her good?
*Yes, sir!*
Did you do like you should?
*Yes, sir!*
Oh, how did you milk her?
*Swish! Swosh! Swish!*

Did that cow die?
*Yes, sir!*
With a pain in her eye?
*Yes, sir!*
Oh, how did she die?
*Uh! Uh! Uh!*

Did the buzzards come?
*Yes, sir!*
For to pick her bones?
*Yes, sir!*
Oh, how did they come?
*Flop! Flop! Flop!*
Flop! Flop! Flop!
*Flop! Flop! Flop!*

*(When the number is over, the children respond with great applause.)*

**BLACK FAIRY**

They are all so beautiful. And Uncle Julius is a darling. Reminds me of Aesop and the Elder we saw in East Afrika.

**QUEEN MOTHER**

Yes, they are alike in many ways. That's because the telling of animal stories has always been a part of our tradition. But do not be deceived by what you see. The children appear happy because they are able to make the most of what little they had. But we cannot forget that these children were slaves, and as such were denied their basic rights as humans.

**BLACK BIRD**

And the same is true of many Blacks today.

**QUEEN MOTHER**

You're quite correct. Many Black children continue to be treated as though they were slaves. That's why they need you, Black Fairy. Not to receive magic but love and understanding.

**BLACK FAIRY**

I'm beginning to see things more clearly, Queen Mother. Oh, how I wish that I had met you and Black Bird earlier.

**BLACK BIRD**

We've met before, Black Fairy. It's just that neither one of us took the time to talk to each other. Sometimes we forget that all Black people are brothers and sisters. We are all children of Afrika. *(begins singing)*

**AFRIKAN CHILDREN**

**We are Black**
**Like a starless night**
**We are children of Afrika**

We are Ebony
Like burnt toast
We are children of Afrika

We are Brown
Like peanut butter
We are children of Afrika

We are Chocolate
Like a candy bar
We are children of Afrika

We are Amber
Like sweet honey
We are children of Afrika

We are Bronze
Like roasted coffee buds
We are children of Afrika

We are one
We are children of Afrika

## BLACK FAIRY

Where do we go now, Queen Mother?

## QUEEN MOTHER

To the streets of Harlem. One of the largest Black communties in the world. Yes, we will go to Harlem and pick up our culture there. *(A cloud of black smoke appears and the three disappear as the scene ends.)*

## ACT THREE: SCENE ONE
## A STREET IN HARLEM (1960)

*(As the scene opens, we see children playing in the street and engaging in various activities: jumping rope, hop scotch, lagging pennies, etc. Queen Mother, Black Bird and Black Fairy appear and begin singing:)*

### STREETS OF HARLEM

The streets of Harlem
Are filled with children

Who make the most of what they have
On dirty sidewalks
They hop, skip and jump
And play in old buildings
That are dumps

Black children of Harlem
Playing in the streets
Black children of Harlem
Who will give them peace?

The streets of Harlem
Are filled with children
Who make the most of what they have
Sometimes they go hungry
And are dressed in old clothes
But one thing they got and that is soul

Little girls with nappy hair
Fat boys with flat noses
Tall girls with skinny legs
These are the children of Harlem
(Refrain)

*(After their singing, they continue to watch the children play. Stagolee appears in his hip manner, dressed in flashy clothes.)*

### STAGOLEE

Well, if it ain't Queen Mother. And looking good as ever. What's happening, baby?

### BLACK FAIRY

How dare you talk to Queen Mother in that manner! Don't you know who she represents?

### QUEEN MOTHER

Oh, that's all right, dear. I've been knowing Stagolee for a long time. He and I are dear friends.

### STAGOLEE

Sure 'nough, Queen Mother. But who is this chick? Trying to put me down like that.

### QUEEN MOTHER

She's a special friend of mine. Meet Black Fairy.

### STAGOLEE

A fairy! You must be kiddin'. This chick don't look like a fairy to me.

### BLACK BIRD

That's because you are comparing her to those other fairies. The white ones.

### STAGOLEE

Yeah, sister Black Bird, I can dig it. Ain't never really seen no Black fairy. Probably wouldn't look so bad if she got her some new rags.

---

## BLACK FAIRY

*(indignantly)* But I'm already wearing rags. Why should I replace rags with rags?

## STAGOLEE

*(laughs)* Baby, are you for real? I'm talking 'bout new clothes. *(to Queen Mother)* Where did this chick come from anyway, Queen Mother?

## QUEEN MOTHER

From Fairyland. She's not used to some of the language that we speak.

## STAGOLEE

Then how can she be a Black fairy if she ain't hip to what we're all about?

## BLACK FAIRY

Must you always be so harsh?

## STAGOLEE

Yeah, baby – I got to be harsh. This is a harsh world we live in. And you got to be harsh to survive. That's why they call me Bad Stagolee. *(begins singing)*

## BAD STAGOLEE

**I'm a bad Stagolee**
**Big and Black**
**I'm a bad Stagolee**
**Big and Black**

**They call me no good**
**'Cause I don't take no crap**
**They call me no good**
**'Cause they think I'm a sap**

I'm a bad Stagolee
Big and Black
I'm a bad Stagolee
Big and Black

Bad is what I've been
Bad is what I am

What people think of me
Don't mean a d---

## BLACK FAIRY

I think I understand what you mean. *(looks at children)* But we must provide them with another alternative.

## STAGOLEE

That won't be easy. I never had a choice to be anything but what I am. *(points at children)* They ain't got no choice either. Unless someone gives them something other than a broken home, dirty clothes and poor schools. I used to be happy like they are now. But as I began to grow up...I learned that unless I took care of myself...no one else would. Maybe you can help some of these children to have more pride in themselves. As for me, I got to space. There's a big crap game coming up, and I feel like it just might be my lucky day. *(kisses Queen Mother on the forehead)* Later, sweetheart. And you too, Black Bird. And Miss Fairy...you look good just like you are, pretty and Black. *(exits)*

## QUEEN MOTHER

Yes, that Stagolee is something. Why, he's already a legend around here. Stagolee talks tough, but he's really not that bad. It's a front he has to put on. He's been kicked around for so long, like many of our Black men. But Stagolee is a real man. A real man, and don't let anyone ever tell you different. Our Black men can be beautiful. And they can also be strong. *(begins singing)*

## BLACK MEN CAN BE BEAUTIFUL

Black men can be beautiful
Black men can be strong
Black men can be wonderful
Even though sometimes they are wrong

Black men helped build this country
When they didn't have much at all
Even when they were treated bad
Most of them stood tall

There was Ole Nat Turner
Who had a vision
To see his people free

There was Frederick Douglass
Who refused to be a slave
And live in misery

There was Marcus Garvey
A strong man
Who believed in Black unity

There was Dr. King
He gave his life for us
He was a man of peace

There was Brother Malcolm X
Who also died
So we could be free


## BLACK FAIRY

I'm sorry I spoke to him the way I did. There's so much more I must learn.

---

## BLACK BIRD
You're doing fine. Isn't she, Queen Mother?

## QUEEN MOTHER
*(nods head)* Yes, she's doing real fine. *(The children see a man carrying a twelve string guitar and cheerfully rush over to greet him. Queen Mother, Black Bird and Black Fairy observe.)*

## FIRST BOY
It's Leadbelly!

## SECOND BOY
Hi ya, Leadbelly.

## GIRL
Won't you sing us a song, Leadbelly?

## LEADBELLY
*(touches the children on their heads)* Well I do declare. If it ain't my favorite friends. Now you know old Leadbelly always does something for his friends. What do you want me to play?

## GIRL
Little Sally Walker!

## LEADBELLY
All right with me. Now supposin' you just kneel down, and the fellows will make a circle round ya. *(The girl kneels in a circle, and Leadbelly begins to sing and play.)*

## LITTLE SALLY WALKER

**Little Sally Walker sitting in a saucer**
**Weeping and moaning like a turtle dove**
**Rise, Sally, rise. Wipe your weeping eyes**

---

Put your hands on your hips
Let your backbone slip
Now shake it to the east
And shake it to the west
Now shake it to the one
Who you like the best

*(The girl selects one of the boys, who in turns kneels in a circle.)*

Little Jimmy Walker sitting in a saucer
Weeping and moaning like a turtle dove
Rise, Jimmy, rise. Wipe your weeping eyes
Turn to the east
Turn to the west
Turn to the one that you love best.

*(After the children play Little Sally Walker, they all sit down, and Leadbelly remains standing.)*

## LEADBELLY

Now I got a real treat for you. I'm gonna let you hear one of my newest songs. It's called "Skip to My Lou." *(The children clap their hands and enthusiastically wait for Leadbelly to begin singing.)*

## LEADBELLY

All right children, it goes something like this.

## SKIP TO MY LOU

Lost my partner, skip to my Lou
Lost my partner, skip to my Lou
Lost my partner, skip to my Lou
Skip to my Lou my darlin'

I'll get another one prettier than you
I'll get another one prettier than you
I'll get another one prettier than you

Skip to my Lou, my darlin'

Hey, hey, skip to my Lou...
Can't get a bluebird, a jaybird'll do....
Little red wagon painted blue
Fly in the sugar bowl, shoo fly, shoo....

My old shoe is torn in two
Cows in the cornfield two by two?
Stole my partner, what'll I do?
I'll get another one quicker than you.
Hey, hey, skip to my Lou.

*(Children clap hands when song is over.)*

### LEADBELLY

All right, children. Now let me hear you say some rhymes.

### FIRST BOY

Ok, I'll be first.

### LEADBELLY

Now you know that ladies are always first. *(motions to the little girl to start the game off)*

### GIRL

*(stands)*

### <u>CHULA, LU!</u>

I'm a big fat lady!
Chula, Lu!
I'm just from the country!
Chula, Lu!
Just outen' the kitchen
Chula, Lu!
With a handful o' biscuits!

Chula, Lu!
You know I wants to marry?
Chula, Lu!
Then, Miss Fancy
Chula, Lu,
Fly way over yonder!
Fly way over yonder!
Now choose your pardner
Chula, Lu!
And swing him around!
Chula, Lu!
I'm a bald head gen'leman,
Chula, Lu!

## FIRST BOY

*(stands and takes his turn)*

## SHOO, FLY, DON'T BOTHER ME

Shoo, Shoo, Shoo, Shoo-fly don't bother me
Shoo, Shoo, Shoo, Shoo-fly don't bother me
Oh, Shoo-fly, don't bother me
Shoo-fly, don't bother me
Shoo-fly, don't bother me
I belong to the bumble bee

## SECOND BOY

*(stands and takes his turn)*

Once upon a time, goose drank wine
Monkey chewed tobacco on the street car line
Street car broke, monkey choke
And that was the end of the monkey joke

## LEADBELLY

Wow, you kids sure are hot today. Well, old Leadbelly gotta be going now. Gotta go back home and write some more songs. *(begins to exit)*

## FIRST BOY

See ya next time, Leadbelly!

## SECOND BOY

And you promise you'll let us hear your new songs. *(The girl just stands and waves goodbye. The children then go back to skipping rope, playing hop skotch, etc.)*

## QUEEN MOTHER

That was Huddie Leadbelly, king of the twelve string guitar and one of the greatest folk blues singers who ever lived.

## BLACK FAIRY

And to think, I never did know that "Little Sally Walker" and "Skip To My Lou" were written by Leadbelly.

## BLACK BIRD

He wrote hundreds of songs, and many of them were for children. Leadbelly simply loved children. It's a shame that he never did gain the recognition he deserved before he died.

## QUEEN MOTHER

Yes, Leadbelly died just six months before his popular song, "Good Night Irene" made the top of the hit parade.

## BLACK FAIRY

Leadbelly wrote "Good Night Irene?" That used to be one of my favorite songs.

---

## QUEEN MOTHER

He was a remarkable man. Even though he served two terms in prison, he never lost his love for people. Leadbelly was a living example of the blues. The blues are a part of our heritage that can never be taken from us. They can be traced back to the early days of slavery where they were influenced by the different chants and cries that many of the Afrikan slaves brought with them to America.

## BLACK FAIRY

Where do we go next, Queen Mother?

## QUEEN MOTHER

Our journey is over. I think that you have seen enough to help you see your own beauty and how it can be used to help others.

## BLACK FAIRY

But I don't know if I can do it alone.

## BLACK BIRD

Of course you can. Queen Mother is right. Our children need you so very much and when you go out tonight, I know that you will make many of them happy. *(begins to sing)*

## <u>BLACK FAIRY</u>

Black Fairy
Black Fairy
When you go out tonight
When you go out tonight

Will you visit Sister Lucy
With the short woolly hair
And tell her she's as pretty
As anyone that's fair

Black Fairy
Black Fairy
When you go out tonight
When you go out tonight

Will you visit Brother Johnny
Who's ashamed because he's black
And help make him proud and strong
So he'll never turn his back

Will you show all Black children
Their community is not all sad
Will you show all Black children
Their community is not all bad

Black Fairy
Black Fairy
Will you visit all Black children
When you come out tonight
Will you visit all Black children
When you come out tonight

*(Black Fairy begins to weep.)*

## QUEEN MOTHER

Remember, dear, you have something that no magic can ever replace. It's not a wand nor does it consist of some simple words. Your magic is yourself. It is you and your total being. It is ANCIENT EGYPT, WEST AFRIKA, THE MIDDLE PASSAGE, THE PLANTATION and it is HARLEM. IT IS BLACK. TRULY BEAUTIFUL AND BLACK. When you go to Fairyland, you have nothing to be ashamed of. You are beautiful and you are Black and that, my dear, is something to be proud of.

## BLACK BIRD

Remember the song I sang to you, Black Fairy? *(Black Fairy wipes her eyes and nods her head.)* That's what you must do. Tell them they are beautiful. *(begins singing)*

## TELL THEM THEY ARE BEAUTIFUL

Tell them they are beautiful
As beautiful as the stars
Tell them they are wonderful
As wonderful as their hearts

O tell them, O tell them
That being Black is nothing to be ashamed of
O tell them, O tell them
That being Black is something to be proud of

Tell them they are beautiful
As beautiful as the trees
Tell them they are tender
As tender as a breeze

O tell them, O tell them
That being Black is nothing to be ashamed of
O tell them, O tell them
That being Black is something to be proud of

*(After the first chorus, Queen Mother joins in and then Black Fairy. The three hold hands and together continue singing. As Black Fairy exits, the Eulogy is sung by the members of the cast.)*

## EULOGY FOR BLACK FAIRY

You have been where no fairies have gone
Now you can help us be so strong
You have seen everything you can see

**Now you can help us be free**
**Your magic is you and your total being**
**Your magic is you and your total being**
**With no magic**

## EPILOGUE
## BEDROOM IN HARLEM TENEMENT

*(It is late night, and Johnny is again finding it difficult to sleep. A bright light flashes, and Black Fairy appears in front of the cot. Johnny awakens and frowns when he sees her.)*

### JOHNNY
Oh, it's you again. Don't you ever give up?

### BLACK FAIRY
At one time I thought of giving up, Johnny, but now I think differently.

### JOHNNY
You mean you done gone out and got some magic?

### BLACK FAIRY
Well no...not the kind you have in mind, Johnny.

### JOHNNY
Then how do you expect to make things better...if you don't have any magic?

### BLACK FAIRY
*(sits on cot)* Well you see, Johnny, there is really no magic in the world that can change some of the things you talked about. But...you can help change them, Johnny, by learning more about your culture and believing in yourself.

### JOHNNY
*(listens more intently)* Yeah...you gotta be jokin'.

### BLACK FAIRY
No, Johnny, it's no joke. Tell me, Johnny, do you know who you really are?

**JOHNNY**

What do you mean? I don't get it.

**BLACK FAIRY**

*(begins singing)*

## <u>HEY BLACK CHILD</u>

Hey Black Child
Do ya know who ya are
Who ya really are

Do ya know you can be
What ya wanna be
If ya try to be
What ya can be

Hey Black Child
Do ya know where ya goin'
Where ya really goin'

Do ya know you can learn
What ya wanna learn
If ya try to learn
What ya can learn

Hey Black Child
Do ya know ya are strong
I mean really strong

Do ya know you can do
What ya wanna do
If ya try to do
What ya can do
Hey Black Child
Be what ya can be
Learn what ya must learn

**Do what ya can do**

**And tomorrow your nation**
**Will be what ya want it to be**

### JOHNNY

*(a smile comes to his face)* You know, Black Fairy...maybe you got something there. Yep...maybe you just might have something.

### BLACK FAIRY

*(embraces Johnny)* Yes, I think so. I think we both have something to be very proud of. *(They continue to embrace as the lights fade out and the play ends.)*

### THE END

# YOUNG JOHN HENRY

# Young John Henry
## A MUSICAL DRAMA FOR CHILDREN IN THREE ACTS

### USENI EUGENE PERKINS

### MUSIC BY WANDA BISHOP

"Young John Henry" was first produced at the LaMont Zeno Theater, Better Boys Foundation Family Center, in February 1976 and was directed by Pemon Rami. Permission for the performance of this play must be obtained from ETA Creative Arts Foundation, Inc., 7558 S. South Chicago Ave., Chicago, IL 60619 – 312/752-3955.

# CHARACTERS
## (In Order of Appearance)

CAP'N JACK (NARRATOR)

OLDER JOHN HENRY (FIGURE)

YOUNG JOHN HENRY

LUCY ANN

MAMA BELLE

POPPA GUS

LIL JANE

UNCLE BUDDY

BIG TANK

MR. JIM CROW

GRANDMA MOSES

LITTLE SONNY

CAPTAIN SMITH

# SONGS

*Traditional John Henry Ballad*

*World is Changing Everyday*

*Gotta See It to Believe It*

*John Henry's Coming Home*

*John Henry Has Come Home*

*I Love You Very Much*

*With a Hamma' in My Han'\**

*Come Along With Me*

*I'm a Steel Driving Man*

*Let's Go to the Picnic*

*We Been in Trouble*

*Nothing But a Man*

*Facts of Life*

*We Are the Dock Workers*

*John Henry is My Name*

*You Did It*

*You Gotta Have Faith*

*If That's the Way*

*With Hamma' in My Han'\**

*Go Along Your Way*

---

\* "With a Hamma' in My Han' " is sung twice in this play.

---

# ACT I

**SCENE ONE:** *A SMALL CABIN ON A FARM IN CHITTLIN'*

*SWITCH, ALABAMA – FRONT PORCH*

**SCENE TWO:** *FRONT PORCH – TWO HOURS LATER*


# ACT II

**SCENE ONE:** *FRONT PORCH – MORNING*

**SCENE TWO:** *NEAR THE CABIN – LATE MORNING*


# ACT III

**SCENE ONE:** *A BUSY DOCK – AFTERNOON*

**SCENE TWO:** *FRONT PORCH – DAY*

# ACT ONE: SCENE ONE

PLACE:      **Farm in Chittlin' Switch, Alabama**
TIME:      **The past**
SETTING:    **A small cabin with a front porch**

*(The scene opens as Cap'n Jack appears on stage, dressed in overalls, holding a guitar. He looks at the audience, smiles and begins thumping his guitar as he sings the traditional "John Henry" ballad. As he sings, a light appears in the background on a figure who is hammering away with a large hammer. The figure is John Henry, as a man, and can be seen through a screen. After completing the ballad, Cap'n Jack walks to the front of the stage, and the light goes out on the figure.)*

## CAP'N JACK

*(gingerly holds his guitar)* Yep, that John Henry sure was a steel driving man if there ever was one. Of course, like the song says, the hammer was the cause of him dying. But John Henry didn't die like no ordinary man. No, siree. That's because he was no ordinary man. He was almost seven feet tall and built like a mountain. Ain't never been a man strong as John Henry. Why, some people declare he was as strong as one hundred oxen. And believe me, they weren't exaggerating one bit. No, siree...not one bit. Why, I saw John Henry do things that defied the imagination. Yes, siree...like the time he worked on the Diamond Joe, a big freight steamer that used to carry cotton up and down the Ole Mississippi. One day, the Diamond Joe got stuck in some heavy sand, and everybody knew the old boat was gonna sink. But John Henry, why he took the boat's anchor and doved into the water and began pulling Diamond Joe outta the sand. Yes, siree. He pulled and pulled until that old boat was in deep water again. *(pauses)* Then there was the time that John Henry rescued fifty miners who were trapped in a coal mine after one of its tunnels collapsed. John Henry got himself to the miners just in the nick of time. Yes, siree.

Yep, John Henry was one strong man. And his legend spread all over Alabama, Mississippi, Tennessee and even to the coast of Georgia. He was a real folk hero – that John Henry. Always wanting to help people. Of course, he wasn't all perfect. But what man is?!! And he had a lot of pride in being Black too. Didn't believe in bowing to no man – not even white folks. Use to always say that "a man ain't nothing but a man." And he was every bit a man...all seven feet and two hundred and ninety pounds. Now, many of you know about John Henry, the man. No doubt, your parents and your grandparents told you about some of the things he did. But how many of you know about young John Henry? Yes, siree...I was right there when he was born back in – er – er...*(scratches his head)* well I can't quite recollect when it was right now. *(smiles)* But I was there alright, in Chittlin' Switch, Alabama, on the farm of Mama Belle and Poppa Gus. They were his parents. I can remember the very day that his mama and Lil Jane, his auntie, brought him home from the hospital. He was so big at birth that Poppa Gus had to make him a bed over four feet long. Yes, siree – over four feet long. There ain't never been a baby born big as John Henry. Like I said – I was right there the day they brought that big strapping boy home. Of course, he had his hammer with him. John Henry was born with a hammer in his hands. Yes, siree...John Henry was born with a hammer in his hands. Just like the song says. *(begins singing)*

## TRADITIONAL JOHN HENRY BALLAD
**When John Henry was a little baby**
**Sitting on his daddy's knee**
**His daddy said, "Look-a-here, John Henry, my boy**
**Be a steel-driving man like me – Lord, Lord!**
**Be a steel-driving man like me"**

**When John Henry was a little baby**
**Sitting on his mama's knee**
**He picked up a hammer and a little piece of steel**
**Said, Hammer be the death of me, oooh weee'**
**Said, Hammer be the death of me**

But to get on with the story...It was early, 'bout 6 p.m. Everybody was waiting around the farm house to see John Henry. There was Poppa Gus, Uncle Buddy, and yes, there was Grandma Moses sitting in her rocking chair on the front porch. *(The lights come on the entire stage, and Cap'n Jack moves back and blends in with the action.)*

### UNCLE BUDDY

*(to Poppa Gus)* I reckon Mama Belle and Lil Jane be comin' home soon. I'm sure anxious to see that boy of yours, Poppa Gus. *(takes a chew of tobacco)* Is he really big as they say? *(Poppa Gus smiles and nods his head.)*

### CAP'N JACK

He's every bit, Uncle Buddy. And maybe a few pounds more.

### UNCLE BUDDY

*(scratches his head)* And is it really true he was born with a hammer in his hand?

### CAP'N JACK

As true as I'm standing here. Ain't that right, Poppa Gus?

### POPPA GUS

It's the truth alright. I was there when he was born. Couldn't believe my eyes at first. But there he was – all thirty pounds of him holding a hammer so big that the doctor was scared to come close to him. *(laughs)* I'm his father – and was a bit scared myself.

### UNCLE BUDDY

*(continues scratching his head)* I'm not one to call a man a liar – especially the boy's father – but I won't believe it till I see it.

### POPPA GUS

Well, you'll be seeing him pretty soon.

### GRANDMA MOSES

*(knitting as she sits in her rockin' chair)* What's he gonna do with a hammer anyway, Poppa Gus? Ain't nothing but cotton round these parts.

### UNCLE BUDDY

*(laughs)* Maybe he's gonna hammer the cotton 'stead of pickin' it.

### POPPA GUS

Don't you worry 'bout what John Henry gonna do. He was born with a hammer in his hand, and I'm sure the good Lord will find something for him to do with it.

### CAP'N JACK

Poppa Gus is right. Why, a boy that strong can do almost anything. And who knows – maybe one of those train companies will be layin' tracks around here one day.

### GRANDMA MOSES

Don't go talking 'bout no trains, Cap'n Jack. We don't need them round here, with all their noise and smoke.

### CAP'N JACK

Whatcha got against trains, Grandma Moses? It's a sign of progress. Got trains running all over the country now.

### GRANDMA MOSES

I still don't like them. Been living 80 years without ever riding in one. Things are alright just the way they are.

### CAP'N JACK

But if we had a train 'round here, we could visit Cousin Leroy and his family in Birmingham and be back in a few days. There ain't nothing like progress, Grandma Moses. Believe me, the world is changing every day. *(begins singing)*

---

## WORLD IS CHANGING EVERYDAY
The world is changing everyday
The world is changing everyday
Things ain't like they use to be
'Cause the world's changing every day

Use to be it would take a week
Just to go to Battle Creek
Now you can get there in one day
By riding a train with no delay
Can't stop progress having its way
Believe me, the train is here to stay
Betta begin to have some patience
'Cause trains are running all over this nation


### GRANDMA MOSES
*(adamant)* I still don't like trains, Cap'n Jack. I like things just the way they are! *(continues knitting)*


### POPPA GUS
*(takes out his pocket watch)* They should be here by now. Wonder what's keeping them?


### UNCLE BUDDY
*(laughs)* If John Henry is big as you claim he is...maybe the wagon done broke down.


### POPPA GUS
That ain't so funny, Uncle Buddy. Why, that wagon has carried over five tons of cotton. Now John Henry may be big – but he ain't that big.


### CAP'N JACK
Not yet, you mean.

---

**POPPA GUS**

Well, you got a point there, Cap'n Jack. I suppose when John Henry grows up to be a young man – we may have to worry a bit. But as for now, John Henry is just a baby – *(pauses and smiles)* even if he does weigh 30 pounds.

**UNCLE BUDDY**

*(laughs)* Who happens to be born with a hammer in his hands. *(scratches his head)* I still got to see it to believe it! *(begins singing)*

### GOTTA SEE IT TO BELIEVE IT
I gotta see it to believe it
Before I'm convinced
I gotta see it to believe it
Before it makes any sense

Now I have seen
Many things in my life
That didn't always
Seem to be right

But I've never seen a baby born
With a hammer in his hand
I've never seen a baby born
With a hammer in his hand

I've seen men climb mountains
As high as the sky
I've seen men swim oceans
In the heaviest of tides

I've seen mighty tornadoes
Whip across the land
I've seen gusty winds
Lift up the sand

---

> But I've never seen a baby born
> With a hammer in his hand
> Lord knows – I've never seen a baby born
> With a hammer in his hand

### CAP'N JACK

*(looks excitedly)* Well, Uncle Buddy – you're 'bout to see one right now. *(places his hand horizontally over his eyes as though he's looking at something afar)* If I ain't mistaken – that's them coming up the road. 'Bout a half mile away.

### POPPA GUS

*(assumes a similar posture next to Cap'n Jack)* Sure 'nough is. That's them alright. I can tell that wagon anywhere. *(Uncle Buddy joins them.)*

### GRANDMA MOSES

*(remains in rocking chair but stretches a bit)* I declare – my grandson's coming home. Sure hope these pajamas are big enough for that boy.

### POPPA GUS

You sure you got everything ready, Cap'n Jack?

### CAP'N JACK

Just like you said, Poppa Gus. Plenty of cider, ginger bread, hot corn and good ole fried chicken.

### UNCLE BUDDY

You mean we gonna have a party...whoopee! *(jumps up and down)*

### POPPA GUS

Of course we gonna have a party. Ain't every day that a man can celebrate an occasion like this. In fact, I invited everyone in the community to come out! *(People begin coming from everywhere and begin exchanging hand shakes in a jubilant manner.)* Make yourselves at home everybody! John Henry's coming home! *(Begins singing)*

<u>JOHN HENRY'S COMING HOME</u>
John Henry's coming home
Be prepared for a surprise
John Henry's coming home
You won't believe your eyes

O, John Henry
O, John Henry
John Henry's comin' home
John Henry's comin' home
(refrain)

*(They all begin to dance and celebrate.)*

**UNCLE BUDDY**

*(raises his hand for silence)* Now listen everybody! I just want you all to know that I'm mighty happy you came out to see John Henry. It makes me feel real good to know that Mama Belle and me got such good neighbors. Now I know many of you have been hearing all kinds of things about John Henry. But let me tell you all this. There ain't nothing wrong with John Henry. Not a thing in the world. He's just a big boy who likes to play with a hammer. *(everybody laughs)* But he's gonna be a good boy, one that all you folks in Chittlin' Switch, Alabama will be mighty proud of. John Henry is gonna be a great man some day. *(Everybody shouts their approval.)* But let me tell you this...he just don't belong to Mama Belle and me. He belongs to all us Black folks! *(Everybody shouts their approval.)* This is a day we'll all remember. Yes, my brothers and sisters, this is a day that the world will never forget. *(Everybody shouts their approval.)* Now there's plenty of chicken, hot corn, apple cider and ginger bread. I want you all to have a good time. *(Everybody rejoices as Grandma Moses holds up a pair of red pajamas.)*

---

## UNCLE BUDDY

*(excitedly)* They're here! John Henry is here! *(Everybody rushes to see John Henry, who is obscured from the audience. They begin dancing and singing again.)*


### JOHN HENRY HAS COME HOME
O, John Henry
O, John Henry
John Henry has come home!
John Henry has come home!
(refrain)

*(They continue to sing and dance as the scene fades out.)*


## ACT ONE: SCENE TWO
## FRONT PORCH: TWO HOURS LATER

*(It is dark, and Poppa Gus and Mama Belle are sitting on the porch. The only light comes from inside the cabin. Cap'n Jack and Lil Jane exit from the cabin.)*


### CAP'N JACK

Well, the little fellow – I mean big fellow – is tucked away. Of course, he had to sleep with that hammer of his in his hand. *(laughs)*


### POPPA GUS

*(looks up and smiles)* I guess Mama Belle and me gonna have to learn to live with that. Thanks for everything, Cap'n Jack. *(Cap'n Jack nods his head.)*

## MAMA BELLE

And you too, Lil Jane. I don't know what I would have done without you.

## LIL JANE

Think nothing of it, dear. And remember, I promised to help with John Henry's diapers or anything else you need done.

## MAMA BELLE

Thank you so much, Lil Jane. I'm sure I can use all the help I can get.

## CAP'N JACK

*(looks at the sky)* Pretty night, ain't it? Never seen the moon so big and bright before.

## POPPA GUS

*(boastfully)* That's 'cause there ain't never been anyone like John Henry before.

## CAP'N JACK

*(laughs)* You can say that again. Well – I guess me and Lil Jane'll be going. Gotta lot of work to do in the morning.

## LIL JANE

*(kisses Mama Belle)* See ya later. *(exits behind Cap'n Jack as Poppa Gus and Mama Belle wave goodbye)*

## MAMA BELLE

Sure was a wonderful party – wasn't it, Poppa Gus?

## POPPA GUS

*(takes her hand)* Yes, Mama Belle. Plenty of good folks 'round here.

## MAMA BELLE

I'm so happy. We have so much to be grateful for.

## POPPA GUS

Yes, the good Lord been mighty kind to us. Mighty kind, indeed. But you know, Mama Belle – the good Lord has been kind to me ever since I met you.

## MAMA BELLE

*(blushes)* You can say the nicest things. John Henry is really lucky to have a father like you. He's gonna be a good boy, you know.

## POPPA GUS

He's already a good boy. Even if he does go round holding a hammer in his hands.

## MAMA BELLE

*(affectionately)* Did I ever tell you how much I love you?

## POPPA GUS

*(pauses)* I suppose so. You must have.

## MAMA BELLE

Well just in case I didn't – let me tell you now.  *(begins singing)*

### <u>I LOVE YOU VERY MUCH</u>
**I love you very much
and that makes me happy
I love you very much
and that makes me glad**

**I love you in the morning
When the sun comes out
I love you in the evening
Without any doubt**

**I love the way you hold my hand
and look me in the eye**

I love the way you speak to me
Whenever you say goodbye

I love you for being a strong Black man
Who is good and kind
I love you most of all
Because you are mine

*(They embrace and kiss as the scene fades out.)*

## ACT TWO: SCENE ONE

*(Cap'n Jack appears, holding his guitar and walks to center stage.)*

### CAP'N JACK

And that's the way it all began. Yes, siree. And from that day on, Chittlin' Switch, Alabama, would never be the same again. Word about John Henry spread all over the county, and people came from everywhere just to see for themselves this magnificent specimen of nature. At first, Poppa Gus, Mama Belle and Grandma Moses were disturbed by the attention John Henry was receiving. But they soon became accustomed to the crowds and were pleased that so many people admired their son. John Henry didn't mind one bit the attention he was receiving and would always welcome visitors with a friendly smile. Of course, he was never without his hammer and would always oblige his admirers with a demonstration of his strength. It seemed like John Henry would never stop growing. Why, when he was five years old, he was over 100 pounds, and when he was ten, he was working in the cotton fields with the other men folk. And John Henry could really pick some cotton. Why, one day he picked over ten tons of cotton and brought it back to the cabin all by himself. It was a good thing too. Poppa Gus became ill, and if it wasn't for John Henry, there wouldn't have been any money to pay the bills. But more than anything else, John Henry loved to play with his hammer. Although he didn't mind picking cotton, deep down inside he wanted to be a steel driving man. Yes...John Henry wanted to be a steel driving man. And after working in the fields all day, you could always see John Henry hammering away with his hammer and singing his favorite song.

### FRONT PORCH: MORNING

*(The stage lights come on and we see John Henry, age 12, hammering a peg in the ground and singing his favorite song. Grandma Moses is in her rocking chair on the porch.)*

## WITH A HAMMA' IN MY HAN'
I was born with a hamma' in my han'
An' I'm goin' to help build this great lan'
An' I'm goin' to climb to fame
'Cause John Henry is my name
An' I was born with a hamma' in my han'

I was born with a hamma' in my han'
An' someday I'm goin' to be a great man
I'm gonna help build railroad tracks
That will stretch for miles and miles
I'm gonna help build railroad tracks
'Cause John Henry is my name

*(After he finishes singing, Grandma Moses claps her hands, and he acknowledges her applause with a big smile and wave of hand. Lucy Ann, age twelve, appears from stage left and speaks to Grandma Moses before going over to where John Henry is.)*

#### LUCY ANN
Want to go on a picnic with the rest of us kids, John Henry?

#### JOHN HENRY
*(He continues to hammer on the peg without looking at her.)* Ain't got no time for picnics, Lucy Ann.

#### LUCY ANN
*(disappointed)* Not even for a little while?

#### JOHN HENRY
*(continues hammering)* No...not even for a little while.

#### LUCY ANN
*(places hands on hips)* But you promised you would go with me this time.

**JOHN HENRY**

*(still hammering)* I'm sorry, Lucy Ann. But I got to keep building up my rhythm. Why, I should've knocked that peg in the ground in three strikes. *(places another peg in the ground and starts hammering on it)*

**LUCY ANN**

Is that all you can ever do, John Henry!

**JOHN HENRY**

Can't think of nothing better to do. Can you?

**LUCY ANN**

I can think of a lot of things that are better.

**JOHN HENRY**

*(stops hammering)* That's cause you just don't understand how important my hammer is to me, Lucy Ann.

**LUCY ANN**

I thought I was important to you, John Henry.

**JOHN HENRY**

Well, er – you are, Lucy Ann. But now, you take this hammer *(holds up hammer)* – it's something that's part of me.

**LUCY ANN**

I know that, John Henry. But I would like to be a part of you too.

**JOHN HENRY**

You are, Lucy Ann.

**LUCY ANN**

You don't act like it. If you did, you would go to the picnic with me. Please, John Henry, why don't you put down your hammer and come along with me! *(begins singing)*

## COME ALONG WITH ME
**Please, John Henry**
**Why don't you put your hammer down**
**Why don't you put your hammer down**
**And come along with me**
**And come along with me**

**Please, John Henry**
**Why don't you forget about that hammer**
**Why don't you forget about that hammer**
**And come along with me**
**And come along with me**

**Please, John Henry**
**A hammer can't be everything**
**A hammer can't be everything**
**So why don't you come along with me**
**So why don't you come along with me**

*(After Lucy Ann completes her song, John Henry begins singing.)*

## I'M A STEEL DRIVING MAN
**Don'tcha know I'm a steel driving man**
**Don'tcha know I'm a steel driving man**
**Gotta nail this peg into the ground**
**Gotta nail this peg into the ground**

**Can't stop hammering**
**'Cause I got work to do**
**Can't stop hammering**
**Until I'm through**

*(Cap'n Jack appears with Uncle Buddy.)*

**CAP'N JACK**

Well, if it ain't my two favorite young people. You two will make a mighty nice couple when you grow up.

**LUCY ANN**

*(indignant)* Do I look like a hammer, Cap'n Jack? That's all John Henry ever cares about.

**CAP'N JACK**

Are you kidding? Ain't no hammer ever looked as pretty as you.

**LUCY ANN**

I bet that ain't what he thinks. *(turns her back and begins to weep)*

**CAP'N JACK**

I'm sure John Henry don't think that. Now do you, John Henry? *(He doesn't respond.)* Well – do you John Henry...?

**JOHN HENRY**

Course I don't. It's just that I'm sorta attached to this here hammer.

**CAP'N JACK**

But a hammer can't fall in love with you, John Henry. Only a woman can do that.

**LUCY ANN**

It won't be me.

**JOHN HENRY**

Don't be like that, Lucy Ann.

**LUCY ANN**

What you expect me to be like when you're always holding that old hammer?

**JOHN HENRY**

I expect you to understand – that I'm a steel driving man.


**CAP'N JACK**

Now don't you two children start arguing! *(Uncle Buddy and Lil Jane appear with lunch baskets.)*


**UNCLE BUDDY**

You all going on the picnic?


**LIL JANE**

Course they are, Uncle Buddy. Ain't that right, Cap'n Jack?


**CAP'N JACK**

*(looks at John Henry and Lucy Ann)* Well, what about it kids...


**JOHN HENRY**

*(puts down his hammer)* Well, I suppose so. If it's alright with you, Lucy Ann. *(She tries to be coy, but finally smiles and nods her approval.)*


**CAP'N JACK**

Then it's all settled. We'll all go to the picnic.


**JOHN HENRY**

Course, I got to take my hammer with me. *(looks at Lucy Ann for her approval)*


**LUCY ANN**

*(affectionately)* Yes, John Henry, you can take your ol' hammer.


**CAP'N JACK**

Then let's all go to the picnic. *(begins singing)*

---

## LET'S GO TO THE PICNIC
Let's go to the picnic
Let's go to the picnic
Let's go to the picnic
So we can have some fun


### LIL JANE

I got the chicken
It's crisp and hot
I got the biscuits
They'll really hit the spot

### UNCLE BUDDY

I got the apple cider
It's sweet and cool
I got the corn on the cob
We'll have plenty of food
(refrain)

*(They all join hands and dance as the scene fades out.)*


## ACT TWO: SCENE TWO

*(Cap'n Jack appears and again walks to the front of the stage to speak to the audience.)*


### CAP'N JACK

Yes, Chittlin' Switch, Alabama would never be the same again. Since the day John Henry was born, it had become one of the most popular places in Alabama. Yes, siree. And John Henry – why, he continued to grow and get bigger. Why, when he was thirteen – he was stronger than most men. As for Poppa Gus and Mama Belle, they had never been happier, and through it all, Grandma Moses would sit in her rocking chair as though she was the proudest person in the world. That is, until Poppa Gus got sick again and wasn't able to work in the fields anymore. And what made matters worst, it hadn't rained in nearly two months, which meant there wasn't any cotton to pick anyway. Now Poppa Gus depended on his cotton crop to pay off the mortgage on his farm. Now the bank that held the mortgage didn't seem to care about Poppa Gus' problem and sent one of its collectors to demand payment. The situation became so serious that the bank threatened to confiscate the land if the payment wasn't made in one month. Yes, siree – Poppa Gus was really in trouble. *(exits off stage)*

## NEAR THE CABIN: LATE MORNING

*(Poppa Gus is standing in front of the cabin talking to the bank collector as Grandma Moses looks on from her rocking chair.)*

### POPPA GUS

I don't know if one month will be enough, Mr. Crow. Even if it rains tomorrow – it will take longer than that for my cotton to grow. Can't you at least make it two months?

### JIM CROW

I'm sorry, Poppa Gus. Business is business. How do you expect our bank to survive if we kept extending credit?

### POPPA GUS

But it's not my fault that it hasn't rained in two months.

### JIM CROW

*(straight faced)* We have nothing to do with the weather. We're in the banking business.

### POPPA GUS

But we've been living here for nearly thirty years. There ain't no other place else for us to go.

---

## GRANDMA MOSES

*(in a loud voice)* That's right, Mr. Crow. And I've been here almost forty years. Now you just have to be patient til we get your money.

## JIM CROW

*(uneasy)* I'm afraid we can't be any more patient, Grandma Moses.

## GRANDMA MOSES

You can if you want to! You white folks got enough land anyway. 'Bout time you show a little consideration for us poor folks. Why, my family have put enough work in this place to have owned it years ago. Now you just go back to that bank of yours and tell them they'll get their money when things get better.

## JIM CROW

*(flabbergasted)* Now I hope you don't start making trouble, Poppa Gus.

## POPPA GUS

We ain't making trouble, Mr. Crow. It's you that's making the trouble.

## GRANDMA MOSES

*(chuckles)* That's telling him, Poppa Gus. But if it's trouble he's looking for – then we ain't ones to run away from it. You bet your life we ain't.

## JIM CROW

I think Grandma Moses got things all wrong, Poppa Gus. Now you better talk to that old woman before you're really in trouble.

## POPPA GUS

Don't tell me 'bout being in trouble. Why, we been in trouble ever since you white folks done put us in slavery. *(begins singing)*

## WE BEEN IN TROUBLE
We been in trouble
Since the day we came here
We been in trouble
Since the day we came here

Use to be we work in the fields
Without any pay
Bend our backs and break our bones
Working throughout the day

Use to be we sweat and toil
And smile and bow our heads
But them days are gone forever
For now we act as men instead

So don't you worry, Mr. Crow
We ain't scared of you no mo'
For we been in trouble
Since the day we were born

*(Mr. Jim Crow exits furiously as John Henry appears.)*

### JOHN HENRY
*(with hammer in hand)* What's wrong with Mr. Jim Crow, Poppa Gus?
Seems like he's plenty mad.

### GRANDMA MOSES
*(boastfully)* That's cause your father told him a thing or two. You did
the right thing, son. Stand up and be a man. *(chuckles)*

### JOHN HENRY
What's Grandma Moses talking about?

**POPPA GUS**

Nothing for you to worry 'bout, John Henry. We're just a little behind on our mortgage, and that fool threatened to take our property.

**JOHN HENRY**

Ain't no one gonna do that, Poppa Gus! Not if I can help it!

**POPPA GUS**

Now don't you worry. Everything will be alright. But it would help a bit if we got some rain. Can't grow cotton without water.

**JOHN HENRY**

*(looks up at the sky)* Sure don't look like its gonna rain soon, Poppa Gus.

**POPPA GUS**

Well, the good Lord will think of something. The bank that Mr. Jim Crow works for does have the right to take our property if we don't pay them in 30 days.

**JOHN HENRY**

Well, if we can't grow any cotton – then I'll get a job someplace else and make some money.

**POPPA GUS**

Where would you go, my boy?

**JOHN HENRY**

To Mobile. There's a lot of boats in the gulf that needs unloading. Why, I probably could unload one of those boats all by myself.

**POPPA GUS**

We wouldn't want you to leave home, son.

## JOHN HENRY

I'm almost a man, Poppa Gus. I can take care of myself. Why, I'll go down to Mobile and make enough money to pay off the whole mortgage. A man ain't nothing but a man. *(begins singing)*

### NOTHING BUT A MAN
**A man ain't nothing but a man**
**And he has to take a stand**
**And do what must be done**
**So victory can be won**

**A man must stand tall**
**No matter what the odds**
**A man cannot fall**
**Even if he's tired**

**A man ain't nothing but a man**
**So don't you worry none**
**Everything will be alright**
**'Cause John Henry is your son**

*(Poppa Gus embraces John Henry.)*

## GRANDMA MOSES

*(jubilant)* That's the spirit, John Henry! That's the spirit!

## POPPA GUS

You got to get permission from Mama Belle first *(John Henry nods his head),* and if she says yes – you promise not to be gone long? *(John Henry nods his head again)* I'm mighty proud of you, son. Mighty proud indeed. I'll go and tell Mama Belle right away. *(exits inside the cabin)*

*(John Henry begins hammering on a peg as Lucy Ann appears.)*

---

**LUCY ANN**

*(hands on hip)* I should've known, hammering on that peg again.

**JOHN HENRY**

*(swings hammer)* Got to build up my muscles. Ain't nothing wrong with that – is it?

**LUCY ANN**

Why do you want to build up your muscles, John Henry? Ain't they big enough now?

**JOHN HENRY**

*(looks at his biceps)* Can't never be too sure. I got a man's job to do – and I wanna make sure I'm up to it.

**LUCY ANN**

What are you talking about?

**JOHN HENRY**

I'm fixin' to go to Mobile and get me a job on the dock loading boats.

**LUCY ANN**

*(surprised)* But what about the farm and your family?

**JOHN HENRY**

That's why I'm going, Lucy Ann. So I can make enough money to pay off the mortgage before the bank takes the property.

**LUCY ANN**

And what about me?

**JOHN HENRY**

Hadn't thought about that. *(Lucy Ann turns her back.)* I didn't mean it like that – only I – er – thought you would understand.

**LUCY ANN**

*(back still turned)* Always taking me for granted.

**JOHN HENRY**

*(smiles)* I knew you'd understand.

**LUCY ANN**

*(faces him)* Don't I always?

**JOHN HENRY**

Yep, a man couldn't ask for a better woman.

**LUCY ANN**

I'm not your woman *(long pause)*, yet!

**JOHN HENRY**

Oh, I know that, Lucy Ann. But someday when I'm famous we're gonna get married. Just as sure as I'm holding this hammer in my hands. *(looks at hammer)*

**LUCY ANN**

Well, if what you say is true – I hope you won't be holding that hammer when we get married.

**JOHN HENRY**

Can't let go my hammer, Lucy Ann. It's what gonna make me famous.

**LUCY ANN**

Ain't never heard of no hammer making anyone famous.

**JOHN HENRY**

*(kisses hammer)* This one will, Lucy Ann. Even if it be the death of me.

---

## LUCY ANN

I don't like you talking that way, John Henry, about that ol' hammer causing your death.

## JOHN HENRY

A man ain't nothing but a man, Lucy Ann...and what's in store for him – is in store for him. *(Mama Belle appears from cabin.)*

## MAMA BELLE

Hello, Lucy Ann. *(Lucy Ann acknowledges her.)* And John Henry – Poppa Gus done told me 'bout you gonna go to Mobile so you can make some money to pay off our mortgage. *(John Henry nods his head.)* That's very fine of you, son. I really don't want you to go – but with Poppa Gus being sick and the weather being what it is – I suppose there's no other choice.

## JOHN HENRY

*(rushes over to Mama Belle and embraces her)* I knew you would understand, Mama Belle.

## GRANDMA MOSES

*(raises her finger)* If John Henry's gonna go to Mobile – you betta prepare him for it, Mama Belle. Mobile ain't nothing like Chittlin' Switch, you know.

## JOHN HENRY

*(confidently)* Don't worry – I can take care of myself. *(flexes his muscles)*

## GRANDMA MOSES

I ain't talking bout how strong you are. There's other things in life a man got to know about.

## MAMA BELLE

But John Henry isn't old enough to learn about the facts of life, Grandma Moses!

## GRANDMA MOSES

*(surprises everyone and rises from her rocking chair)* What do you mean – he ain't old enough! If he's old enough to go down there to Mobile – he's old enough to know about the facts of life. *(points finger at John Henry)* Now you looka here, John Henry. What I'm about to tell you is something that you must never forget – especially when you're in Mobile. Now listen here – you gotta know the facts of life. *(begins singing)*

<u>FACTS OF LIFE</u>
**You got to know
The facts of life
If you expect to survive
For if you don't
You may find yourself
Being eaten up alive**

**You got to know
Who to trust
And who to stay away from
For if you don't
You may find yourself
Always being on the run**

**You got to know
Good from bad
And beware of strangers
For if you don't
You may find yourself
In some real danger**

So take my advice
And keep alert
No matter what you do
Cause the facts of life
Will catch up with you


**JOHN HENRY**

I'll try and remember what you said, Grandma Moses. *(Grandma Moses returns to her rocking chair.)*


**LUCY ANN**

And be careful of those evil women!


**MAMA BELLE**

*(places arm around John Henry)* I know you'll be alright, John Henry. You're a good boy, and the Lord will surely watch over you. But don't forget – you promise to come back in one month.


**JOHN HENRY**

I'll be back. And I'll have enough money to pay off the whole mortgage.


**LUCY ANN**

*(jokingly)* You betta come back, John Henry. If you know what's good for you.


**JOHN HENRY**

*(smiles)* Yes, Miss Lucy Ann. Like Grandma Moses said – I got to learn about the facts of life...don't I!! *(takes her hand as the scene fades out)*

# ACT THREE: SCENE ONE

*(Cap'n Jack appears again and walks to the front of the stage.)*

## CAP'N JACK

And so, John Henry left Chittlin' Switch to go down to Mobile to get a job loading boats. Now, the docks were known to have some of the toughest guys around, and often the men would spend more time fighting against each other than loading the boats. A man really had to be a man to work on the docks around Mobile, Alabama, which John Henry was soon to find out. *(exits off stage)*

## A BUSY DOCK: AFTERNOON

*(A dock along the Gulf in Mobile, Alabama. Men are busy at work and singing as John Henry appears with his hammer in one hand and a small sack in another. He stands and watches the men go through their chores as they continue singing.)*

## <u>WE ARE THE DOCK WORKERS</u>
**We are the dock workers**
**And we are strong**
**'Cause to work on the docks**
**You need plenty meat on your bones**

**We load the ships**
**That will sail up the way**
**Taking all sorts of cargo**
**From Mobile to L.A.**

**We are the men**
**That get things done**
**There's plenty of work**
**But we still have time for fun**

---

And to get a job here
You have to be strong
'Cause you can't work on the docks
Unless you've plenty meat on your bones

*(Little Sonny appears with a large sack of wheat on his shoulder and accidently bumps into John Henry. Little Sonny falls down, spilling the wheat in the process.)*

### JOHN HENRY

*(apologetically)* Please forgive me. *(extends out his arm)* I hope I didn't cause too much damage.

### LITTLE SONNY

*(wipes himself and looks at the spilled wheat)* Well, I suppose it could be worst. *(begins to put spilled wheat back into sack)*

### JOHN HENRY

*(kneels to help him)* Let me help you.

### LITTLE SONNY

*(surprised)* Why thanks – er – what's your name, boy?

### JOHN HENRY

*(proudly)* John Henry...what's yours?

### LITTLE SONNY

*(continues to pick up wheat)* Just call me Little Sonny. You new round here, ain'tcha? *(John Henry nods his head.)* I thought so. When you asked to help me pick up this wheat – I knew you must be new. You know – every man 'round here suppose to take care of himself.

### JOHN HENRY

Where I come from – we believe in helping one another.

**LITTLE SONNY**

Where's that?


**JOHN HENRY**

Chittlin' Switch.


**LITTLE SONNY**

Chittlin' Switch – why ain't that where Uncle Buddy lives...*(stops picking up wheat)*


**JOHN HENRY**

That's right. He's my uncle.


**LITTLE SONNY**

Well I'll be...so you the youngen been hearing so much about. They tell me you're strong as an ox, boy.


**JOHN HENRY**

*(smiles)* Don't know 'bout that. Ain't never seen an ox.


**LITTLE SONNY**

*(looks John Henry over)* You look like you can take care of yourself. But what are you doing down here?


**JOHN HENRY**

Looking for a job.


**LITTLE SONNY**

Boy, you must be crazy! Why, if the work don't get the best of you – the fighting will.


**JOHN HENRY**

Ain't scared of no work...figure I can do as much as the next man – or maybe more.

**LITTLE SONNY**

Jobs are plenty scarce – you know.

**JOHN HENRY**

I only know I got to get me a job so I can pay off the mortgage on my Poppa's and Mama's house.

**LITTLE SONNY**

Sure wish I could help you. Like to see a young fella do something for his folks. *(Captain James appears.)*

**CAPTAIN JAMES**

*(angrily)* What's that wheat doing on the ground?! And who gave you permission to socialize while you're working!

**LITTLE SONNY**

*(politely)* I'm sorry, Captain James. I dropped the sack by accident.

**CAPTAIN JAMES**

You know that will be taken out of your pay. Don't believe in shipping out dirty wheat 'round here. *(Little Sonny begrudgingly nods his head.)* And who is this boy? *(Looks at John Henry)*

**LITTLE SONNY**

His name is –er –

**JOHN HENRY**

I can speak for myself. My name is John Henry.

**CAPTAIN JAMES**

Is that so? *(looks at John Henry's hammer)* And just what are you gonna do with that hammer? This is the docks – not the railroads.

**JOHN HENRY**

I can see that. But I need a job right away – so I came down here.


**CAPTAIN JAMES**

*(laughs)* We ain't got no jobs for boys. This is man's work.


**JOHN HENRY**

*(seriously)* I am a man...Nothing but a man. If you give me a job – I'll show you.


**CAPTAIN JAMES**

You'll show me what?


**JOHN HENRY**

That I can load one of those boats all by myself and faster than all the men you got working here. *(Some of the other dockmen begin to stop and listen as John Henry sings.)*


<u>**JOHN HENRY IS MY NAME**</u>
**I can load any boat on this dock**
**'Cause when I work I never stop**
**Until my job has been done**
**And I will challenge anyone**

**'Cause my name is John Henry**
**John Henry is my name**
**'Cause my name is John Henry**
**John Henry is my name**

**I can do almost anything**
**Once I make up my mind**
**I can get any job done**
**And always complete it on time**

**'Cause my name is John Henry**
**John Henry is my name**

'Cause my name is John Henry
John Henry is my name

*(The other dockmen stand around and watch.)*

## CAPTAIN JAMES
You talk pretty big for a newcomer. I wonder if you're strong enough to back up what you say you can do.

## JOHN HENRY
*(smiles)* Why don't you try me and find out?

## CAPTAIN JAMES
Maybe I will. In fact, it may give the rest of the boys something to laugh about.

## LITTLE SONNY
*(softly)* Don't be a fool, John Henry. No man can load one of these boats by himself. *(A large man steps out from the crowd.)*

## BIG TANK
That's right, Little Sonny. Can't no man load one of those boats by himself. I should know. I tried it once myself.

## JOHN HENRY
*(whispers to Little Sonny)* Who's he?

## LITTLE SONNY
*(softly)* That's Big Tank, the meanest and strongest man on the docks.

## JOHN HENRY
I happen to disagree with you, Big Tank. *(Everyone looks surprised.)*

## BIG TANK
*(steps in front of John Henry)* Are you calling me a liar, boy!

## JOHN HENRY

*(calmly)* I'm not calling you anything. But I know what I can do.

## BIG TANK

Didn't I tell you boy! I tried to load one of those boats myself – and if Big Tank couldn't do it – no man can. *(looks around for approval)* Ain't you ever heard of Big Tank...the strongest man in Alabama?...and maybe the whole country...

## JOHN HENRY

*(politely)* No, I ain't never heard of you, Big Tank. *(Big Tank looks disturbed.)*

## BIG TANK

Well, you have now! And nobody makes a fool out of Big Tank. *(begins to roll up his sleeve)*

## JOHN HENRY

*(holds his position)* I don't want to fight you, Big Tank. But I'm a man just like you, and I don't believe in backing off to anyone. *(Big Tank begins to move toward John Henry, but Captain James inter-venes.)*

## CAPTAIN JAMES

*(stands between John Henry and Big Tank)* I don't want no fighting on the job. You do that on your own time. Now, the only way for us to find out if this boy is only full of wind – is to let him try. *(The other men nod their approval.)* O.K., boy...*(points)* you see what you can do with it. There's plenty sacks of wheat to put on that boat. Are you ready?

## JOHN HENRY

Like I told you, Captain James, I came here to work. *(John Henry quickly begins to carry sacks of wheat to the ship. As he does, the men begin to place bets, and John Henry continues to go back and forth carrying sacks of wheat to the ship. The betting increases as John Henry makes trip after trip, carrying each sack as though it was as light as a feather. He begins to carry two sacks, and then three. Now the men are shouting and clapping in his favor. John Henry continues to load the ship amid a pandemonium-like atmosphere until there is only one sack left. By this time, John Henry is almost exhausted, but manages to retrieve the last sack as the men applaud him on...except for Big Tank.)*

### LITTLE SONNY

*(jumping up and down)* That's it, John Henry! You're on the last one. Stick with it, John Henry! Stick with it! *(John Henry places the last sack on the boat and staggers back to the dock to the jubilant cries of the other men. He manages to reach Little Sonny and then tumbles to the ground. Little Sonny goes to his aid.)* You did it, John Henry! You did it! *(John Henry smiles and stands up slowly as Little Sonny begins to sing.)*

### <u>YOU DID IT</u>
**You did it, John Henry
You did it
You loaded the boat
and won
You did it, John Henry
You did it
And none thought it could be done**

*(Everyone, except Big Tank and Captain James, begin dancing and singing the same song.)*

### BIG TANK

*(holds up his hands and speaks in an angered voice)* Hold it, everyone! Hold it! *(Everyone stops.)* I'm still the strongest man around here – and John Henry has to beat me to prove otherwise.

## LITTLE SONNY
But he won fair and square, Big Tank.

## BIG TANK
*(pushes Little Sonny aside)* Don't you know betta than to say anything when I'm talking! Now as for you, John Henry, we'll see just how much of a man you really are! *(walks slowly towards John Henry who is still tired, but holds his ground)*

## CAPTAIN JAMES
*(nervously)* Why don't you two have an arm wrestling contest? No use of fighting and risking getting hurt. Why, if you two were to tangle at it – who knows what might happen!

## JOHN HENRY
That's fine with me. I don't see no sense of fighting anyway.

## BIG TANK
*(looks around at the other men and sees that they approve of the arm wrestling contest)* Alright, if that's the way you want it! *(Little Sonny brings a box and places it between Big Tank and John Henry. The two men then kneel, lock hands and begin the contest. As they try to move each other's arm, the other men begin shouting and placing bets again. The contest goes on and on, with each man using his ultimate strength until finally John Henry, in a great show of reserve, wrestles Big Tank down.)*

## LITTLE SONNY
*(jumping up and down)* Whoopee! Whoopee! John Henry won! *(Big Tank rises and looks John Henry straight in the eye.)*

## BIG TANK
I got to give it to you, boy. You the strongest man I ever did see. *(pats John Henry on the back)* And a darn gentleman at that.

---

## JOHN HENRY

*(smiles)* You not such a bad guy yourself, Big Tank. Why in another second – I might have lost.

## BIG TANK

*(puts his arm around John Henry's neck as the other men go back to work)* You know, boy – you and me could make a real good team. Why, between the two of us, we could load so many boats that we could make enough money to buy our own. What about it, John Henry?

## JOHN HENRY

Thanks for the offer, Big Tank, but I ain't meant to be no dock worker. *(picks up his hammer)* I'm a steel driving man. Got to get me a job on the railroad some day. I'm just itching to lay me some tracks. Soon as I get enough money, I'm going back to Chittlin' Switch and pay off the mortgage on my folks' property. Then I'll be off to get me a job on the railroad.

## BIG TANK

If that's the way you want it. Too bad, though – we could've really made some kind of team. *(Captain James appears with a roll of bills.)*

## CAPTAIN JAMES

This is your money, John Henry. You made more in one day than most men make in a month. Now maybe you and I can get together and draw up a contract.

## JOHN HENRY

*(counting money)* Don't need to stay any longer. Why, it's enough money here to pay off the whole mortgage.

## CAPTAIN JAMES

*(surprised)* You mean you're going home!

## JOHN HENRY

That's right!

## CAPTAIN JAMES

But you can't do that. Why, you can make a fortune here.

## JOHN HENRY

*(shows Captain James his hammer)* I'm a steel driving man, Captain James. When I make my fortune – it will be from driving steel to hold down those railraod tracks that'll be running all over this country. Yes, sir – I got to help build the railroad.

## CAPTAIN JAMES

*(scratches his head)* If that's what you want to do, John Henry – then I wish you all the luck in the world.

## JOHN HENRY

*(smiles)* Don't need luck, Captain James. All I need is my hammer. *(Little Sonny appears.)*

## LITTLE SONNY

*(excitedly)* Don't forget to say hello to your Uncle Buddy for me. *(John Henry nods his head again.)*

## JOHN HENRY

I'll be sure to tell him, Little Sonny. *(extends his hand out to Big Tank)* Goodbye, Big Tank. See you all! *(waves to the men and they wave back as the scene fades out)*

## ACT THREE: SCENE TWO

## CAP'N JACK

Yes, siree, that was some feat John Henry performed that day in Mobile. And before he could get back home, everyone in Chittlin' Switch had heard about what he had done. And as you'd expect, when the story got back to Chittlin' Switch, it had John Henry loading five

---

boats in less than one hour. Yes, siree. Everyone seem to be alright now that John Henry had earned enough money to pay back the bank, that is except for one thing. While John Henry was away, Mr. Jim Crow discovered that the land the bank was renting to Poppa Gus for all these years had oil on it. Now Mr. Crow had a plan to get that oil. So on the day he went to collect the rent, he had a surprise which you will soon find out about. Like I told you – I was right there when it happened. *(exits off stage)*

## FRONT PORCH: DAY

*(Lights come on Mr. Crow, who is standing next to Poppa Gus and Mama Belle in front of the cabin. Grandma Moses looks on from her rocking chair.)*

### POPPA GUS

*(counts money and hands it to Mr. Jim Crow who looks surprised)* Forty – fifty – sixty – seventy – eighty – ninety – one hundred dollars. Count it yourself to be sure, Mr. Crow.

### MR. JIM CROW

*(begins counting money)* Yes, it's one hundred dollars alright. I really didn't think you would be able to make it on time.

### MAMA BELLE

*(smiles)* That's because you played us cheap, Mr. Crow. Never play Black folks cheap when they put their minds to something that's important to them.

### GRANDMA MOSES

That's telling the old crow! But to tell the truth – I wasn't gonna leave even if we didn't get the money. Now what do you think about that, Mr. Crow! *(laughs)*

## POPPA GUS

No use agitating the man, Grandma Moses. We done paid our debt. That's the only thing that matters. And now that we are getting rain again and I'm feeling a heap bit better – we won't be getting behind in our payments anymore. Now if you don't mind Mr. Crow – I think it best you be leaving. John Henry will be coming back soon – and I don't think he takes a liken to you.

## GRANDMA MOSES

He ain't the only one – if you ask me!

## MAMA BELLE

*(goes to Grandma Moses)* Take it easy, Grandma. Like Popppa Gus said – we done paid our debt.

## MR. JIM CROW

*(nervously)* I'm afraid there's another matter we must settle, Poppa Gus.

## POPPA GUS

What you mean – another matter! You got your money. I don't think we got anything else to discuss.

## MR. JIM CROW

*(holds up his hands)* It's not that simple, Poppa Gus. You see, the bank always maintains an option to redeem its property if it sees fit to do so.

## POPPA GUS

What you mean – redeem your property!

## MAMA BELLE

*(comes to Poppa Gus' side)* Yes – I don't quite understand what you mean either, Mr. Crow.

## MR. JIM CROW

*(tries to be firm but his nervousness still shows)* Well, let me explain. As your landlord, we have every right to take back your property. There never was a lease signed and my bank has instructed me to give you a two day notice.

## GRANDMA MOSES

A two day notice for what!

## MR. JIM CROW

To, er – move. Now, we'll be happy to help you find another place. In fact, we'll even give you your one hundred dollars back. *(takes money out of his pocket)*

## POPPA GUS

Sounds fishy to me, Mr. Crow. Real fishy.

## GRANDMA MOSES

It sure do, Poppa Gus. If you ask me – I smell a skunk. And I don't mean one with four legs.

## MR. JIM CROW

*(trying to be reconcilitory)* Of course you could buy the land yourself if you had two thousand dollars. But then you would have to pay it in two days. After that the land belongs to the bank. It's all legal and on paper. *(Poppa Gus looks dejected.)*

## MAMA BELLE

You know we don't have two thousand dollars.

## MR. JIM CROW

I'm sorry – but the law is the law. *(Uncle Buddy enters in an exuberant manner.)*

## UNCLE BUDDY

Whoopee! Whoopee! You'll all be rich! *(jumps up and down)*

## POPPA GUS

Whatcha talking about, Uncle Buddy?

## UNCLE BUDDY

*(still cannot hold back his excitment)* There's oil on your land, Poppa Gus. I heard some people at the bank talking about it this morning. You got oil on this land. *(begins jumping up and down again)* Whoopee! Whoopee!

## POPPA GUS

*(moves angrily toward Mr. Jim Crow)* So that's why the bank wants this land! *(raises his hand)* Why, I ought to...*(Mama Bell intervenes before he can hit Mr. Jim Crow who backs away, holding his hand over his face.)*

## MAMA BELLE

He's not worth hitting and goin' to jail for. *(restrains Poppa Gus)*

## GRANDMA MOSES

*(rises from her chair and appears to go after Mr. Crow)* Well – he may not be worth hitting – but I'm going to do it anyway. *(She is restrained by Uncle Buddy.)*

## MR. JIM CROW

Now, I have taken enough from all of you. Yes – there's oil on this land – but unless you come up with two thousand dollars in two days and pay for it outright – the bank will take it over. *(begins to laugh)* The joke is really on you all. You're standing on enough money to get you two thousand dollars and much more. But there's no way in the world you can drill an oil well in two days. *(continues laughing)* That's all I have to say. Now good day! *(departs with a feeling of elation as John Henry and Lucy appear)*

---

## JOHN HENRY

I've never seen Mr. Crow look that happy before. Grandma Moses must have said something nice to him for a change. *(looks around and sees that everyone is gloomy)*

## LUCY ANN

*(gets the same feeling)* I don't think she did, John Henry. Judging by the way everyone looks, something seriously wrong must have happened.

## JOHN HENRY

*(rushes to Mama Belle)* What happened! Didn't I make enough money to pay off the debt? *(Poppa Gus turns his back, and Lucy Ann goes to him.)*

## MAMA BELLE

You made enough money, John Henry. But now the bank wants to reclaim its property. *(begins to sob)*

## JOHN HENRY

Why would it want to do that?

## GRANDMA MOSES

'Cause there's oil on it, son. All this time there was oil under our feet. I declare!

## UNCLE BUDDY

That's right, John Henry. I heard about it today at the bank.

## POPPA GUS

If only we could dig a well in two days. Then we could sell the oil and buy the land ourselves.

**JOHN HENRY**

I don't understand, Poppa Gus.

**MAMA BELLE**

What your poppa means is that we still got two days rent left, and if we came up with the money, we could pay for the land.

**JOHN HENRY**

Then that's what we'll do. Come up with the money.

**UNCLE BUDDY**

How are we gonna do that?

**JOHN HENRY**

*(proudly holds up his hammer)* With my hammer – that's how.

**UNCLE BUDDY**

*(in disbelief)* That's impossible!

**POPPA GUS**

Uncle Buddy's right, John Henry. Why drill an oil well it would take a machine nearly a month to do?

**JOHN HENRY**

*(smiles)* Me and my hammer can do the job. *(begins displaying his hammer)*

**LUCY ANN**

John Henry, dear – I know you can do almost anything you set your mind to do. But to dig a well in two days with a hammer – why – that's er – er – crazy.

**JOHN HENRY**

I'm not crazy, Lucy Ann.

## LUCY ANN

I didn't mean it that way. *(goes to John Henry and embraces him)* But I love you so much – I just don't want anything to happen to you.

## JOHN HENRY

*(boastfully)* Ain't nothing gonna happen to me. Now step aside – 'cause I gotta start digging. Ain't got but two days, you know. *(Begins pounding his hammer vigorously against the ground. Everyone looks on in awe as he sings the following song.)*

## <u>YOU GOTTA HAVE FAITH</u>

**If there's oil in the ground
It will sure be found
For me and my hammer
Are gonna pound and pound**

**You gotta have faith
You gotta have faith**

**I'll hammer in the morning
When the sun is hot
I'll hammer in the evening
Til I hit the right spot**

**You gotta have faith
You gotta have faith**

**And when I find that spot
I'll hammer all day
Make a hole so deep
That it's bound to pay**

*(As John Henry hammers and hammers, the spotlight shows on him and changes from bright to dim to suggest that he's been working night and day. On the second evening, Lucy Ann appears while John Henry is still hammering away.)*

**LUCY ANN**

I wish you'd please stop, John Henry. It's been over a day and a half.


**JOHN HENRY**

*(slows his pace a little)* I can't stop, Lucy Ann.


**LUCY ANN**

But you haven't eaten.


**JOHN HENRY**

*(continues hammering)* Ain't had time to eat. Gotta dig this oil well before tomorrow morning.


**LUCY ANN**

I brought you something to eat anyway. *(places a small package on the ground next to John Henry)*


**JOHN HENRY**

*(begins hammering harder than ever)* If I can find a second to take a bite. Thanks.


**LUCY ANN**

I love you, John Henry. *(begins to weep)*


**JOHN HENRY**

I love you too, Lucy Ann. *(She departs as he picks up his pace and continues to hammer away until he finally strikes oil.)* I did it! I did it! I struck oil! I struck oil! *(Poppa Gus and Mama Belle come running out of the cabin as he begins jumping around.)* We don't have to move. There's enough oil here to get us more than two thousand dollars.


**MAMA BELLE**

*(embraces John Henry)* God bless you, John Henry. God bless you.

---

## POPPA GUS

*(on his knees inspecting the ground)* It's oil, alright. Black as a starless night and slippery as Mama Belle's fat back. *(stands)* Wait til that Mr. Crow comes this morning. Why, he'll be so surprised – he'll change his color. *(They all hold hands and begin to celebrate as the scene ends.)*


## ACT THREE: SCENE THREE

*(Cap'n Jack reappears.)*


## CAP'N JACK

*(in his usual affable manner)* Well now, Mr. Jim Crow didn't change his color *(laughs)* – but he sure 'nough changed his job. Yes, siree. The bank got rid of him after he failed to get the land from Poppa Gus and Mama Belle. After paying for the land, they still had enough oil left to buy a little country store. They were really happy. Of course by this time John Henry had become a legend. He was a real folk hero to everyone in these here parts, and stories about him were being told all over the country. But despite all his fame, John Henry was still restless because he had not fullfilled his greatest ambition – to work on the railroad. Finally, his restlessness got the best of him.  When he reached his 18th birthday, he was determined to strike out on his own – to find a job with one of the big railroad companies. I remember the day when he was telling Lucy Ann about his plans. It was one of those hot, humid afternoons when all a person wants to do is stretch out and drink some ice cold lemonade. *(exits off stage)*


## FRONT PORCH: AFTERNOON

*(John Henry and Lucy Ann are standing in front of the cabin. Grandma Moses is asleep in her rocking chair.)*

## LUCY ANN
*(sadly)* I guess I always knew this day would be coming.

## JOHN HENRY
*(takes her hand)* Don't take it so hard, Lucy Ann. Like I said – I'll send for you soon as I get my feet on the ground.

## LUCY ANN
I wish I could go with you now.

## JOHN HENRY
Not a chance! I'll probably be doing a lot of traveling at first and wouldn't want to place no hardships on you.

## LUCY ANN
It wouldn't be a hardship. I love you, John Henry.

## JOHN HENRY
*(chokes a little)* And I love you, too, Lucy Ann. You're the only woman I ever cared for. But when we get married – we'll have our own little place and won't be living outta some suitcase.

## LUCY ANN
*(tries to smile)* Well – if that's the way it must be. *(begins to sing)*

### IF THAT'S THE WAY
If that's the way
It must be
For you to be my man

If that's the way
It must be
I'll try to understand

If that's the way
It must be
For you to come to me

If that's the way
It must be
I'll just wait and see

If that's the way
It must be – John Henry
I will always be true
If that's the way
It must be – John Henry
I will wait for you


**JOHN HENRY**

You'll never regret it, Lucy Ann. For someday I'm going to be famous
and make you really proud of me.


**LUCY ANN**

I'm already proud of you, John Henry.


**JOHN HENRY**

I mean really proud! When I start working on the railroad, this whole
country gonna hear about John Henry. *(begins singing)*


**<u>WITH A HAMMA' IN MY HAN'</u>**
I was born with a hamma' in my han'
An' I'm goin' to help build this great lan'
An' I'm goin' to climb to fame
'Cause John Henry is my name

I was born with a hamma' in my han'
An' someday I'm goin' to be a great man
I gonna help build railroad tracks

That will stretch from miles and miles
I gonna help build railroad tracks


**GRANDMA MOSES**

*(awakens suddenly)* Is that all you can talk about is railraods, John Henry! *(nods his head)* I declare! *(shakes her head)*

**LUCY ANN**

See, I'm not the only one who thinks like this, but since you done made up your mind – I'll accept things the way they are.

*(Uncle Buddy and Lil Jane appear.)*

**UNCLE BUDDY**

*(jovially)* I hear you gonna go and get a job with one of those railroad companies, John Henry.

**JOHN HENRY**

Yes sir, Uncle Buddy. *(holds up his hammer)* Me and this hammer gonna make history.

**LIL JANE**

We're sure gonna miss you, John Henry. You're just like my own child.

**JOHN HENRY**

I'll miss you too, Lil Jane. But a man ain't nothing but a man – and he got to do what he got to do.

**LIL JANE**

I suppose you're right. I found out a long time ago – when a man makes up his mind – there ain't much no one can do. *(hands him a bag)* I made you some cookies to take with you.

### JOHN HENRY

*(kisses Lil Jane on her cheeks as he accepts the bag)* Now you gonna almost make me cry.

### UNCLE BUDDY

Didn't think we let you go without giving you something...*(Mama Belle and Poppa Gus appear. Mama Belle carries a large bag.)*

### MAMA BELLE

Well, son – I put all your clothes in this here bag. Packed them real neat. *(John Henry takes bag and kisses her.)*

### POPPA GUS

Now, don't you forget to let us know what you're doing, John Henry. You ain't never too big to remember your parents. *(John Henry nods his head.)* I suppose its bout time you be leaving, son. *(puts his arm around John Henry)*

### JOHN HENRY

Where's Cap'n Jack? *(Cap'n Jack appears with other neighbors.)*

### CAP'N JACK

Here I am, John Henry! You didn't think I would miss seeing you before you left, now did you!

### JOHN HENRY

Well – I suppose not. *(Everyone mills around John Henry and wishes him good luck.)*

### CAP'N JACK

*(holds up his hands)* Alright everyone – let's all join in and give John Henry a big send off. *(begins singing)*

## GO ALONG YOUR WAY
I wish you all the luck, John Henry
As you go along your way
I wish you the best of everything
And hope you'll be back some day

O, John Henry
O, John Henry
John Henry is going away
John Henry is going away

## LIL JANE

I wish you the best of health, John Henry
As you go along your way
I wish you all the happiness
And hope you be back some day

## GRANDMA MOSES
*(to everybody's surprise, rises and joins the others)*

Now don't you forget your manners, son
As you go along your way
Remember to be a gentleman
And I hope you come back some day

*(Everyone continues to sing and dance as John Henry begins to leave and scene fades out. Cap'n Jack reappears.)*

## CAP'N JACK
The rest is all history. How John Henry got a job on the railroad and became the most famous steel drivin' man the world ever did see. This country could never have been built without the likes of a John Henry. Yes, siree. And when the railroad people wanted to dig a tunnel

---

through the mountain known as Big Bend – the first man they contacted was John Henry. Now Big Bend was one of the hardest mountains in the land, and folks thought the railroad people were crazy thinking they could tunnel through it. But with the help of John Henry and other great steel drivers, they made a tunnel which was claimed to be one of the Seven Wonders of the World. Yes, siree. Of course, John Henry and Lucy Ann finally got married. Sure was a beautiful wedding they had. Folks come to attend from all over the country. And after they were married, John Henry and Lucy Ann were mighty happy together. But then John Henry got the urge to use his hammer again. He had heard of a new steam drill that could out drill any man. John Henry refused to believe this and challenged the machine to a contest. *(bows his head)* You all know what happened next. Yes, siree, that machine and John Henry went against each other like the whole world was at stake. Yes, siree. Ain't no man ever put up a harder struggle than John Henry did against that steam drill. Yes, siree. *(begins singing the traditional John Henry ballad as a large figure of John Henry (the adult) reappears in the background, hammering away with his large hammer. This action continues until the ballad is over and the scene fades out as the play comes to an end.)*

## THE END

# THE LEGEND OF DEADWOOD DICK

# The Legend of
# Deadwood Dick

## A MUSICAL DRAMA FOR CHILDREN IN THREE ACTS

USENI EUGENE PERKINS

MUSIC BY EARNEST McCARTY

"The Legend of Deadwood Dick" was first produced at the ETA Creative Arts Foundation in December 1986 and was directed by Kemati Janice Porter. Permission for the performance of this play must be obtained from ETA Creative Arts Foundation, Inc., 7558 S. South Chicago Ave., Chicago, IL 60619 – 312/752-3955.

# CHARACTERS
## (In Order of Appearance)

**GRANDPA MARCUS**

**BILLY BOY**

**TOPHAT**

**BARTENDER JOE**

**OLDTIMER**

**DEADWOOD DICK**

**CLEOPATRA**

**MISSISSIPPI MOUNTAIN**

**ISAIAH DORMAN**

**CHEROKEE BILL**

**BEN**

**LILLIE**

**WYATT EARP**

**LULU BELLE**

**COWBOYS**

**COWGIRLS**

**MUSICIANS (FIDDLER AND GUITAR PLAYER)**

# SONGS

*The Cattle Drive*

*Cleopatra's Saloon*

*They Call Me Cleopatra*

*I'm a Cow Puncher*

*Gold, Gold!*

*Never Told a Lie*

*It's Been Peaceful*

*Could Be, But Is She?*

*I'm Cherokee Bill*

*Sometimes a Woman*

*He's Gonna Be Free*

*Do Yourself a Favor*

*I May Not Be a Cowboy*

*I Got My Hopes*

*I'm Not the Kind of Man*

*I Feel Like a Queen*

*I'll Be Your King*

*Learn to Love Each Other*

*ACT I*

*SCENE ONE: FRONT PORCH OF A SMALL BUNGALOW IN*

*CHICAGO, ILLINOIS – PRESENT*

*SCENE TWO: CLEOPATRA'S SALOON – AROUND 1870*


*ACT II*

*SCENE ONE: FRONT PORCH – PRESENT*

*CLEOPATRA'S SALOON – AROUND 1870*


*ACT III*

*SCENE ONE:  FRONT PORCH – PRESENT*

*SCENE TWO:  CLEOPATRA'S SALOON – AROUND 1870*

*SCENE THREE:  FRONT PORCH – PRESENT*

# ACT ONE: SCENE ONE

TIME:    **Present**
PLACE:  **Front porch of small bungalow in Chicago, Illinois**

*(Lights on Grandpa Marcus, who is seated in his rocking chair. As he prepares his pipe to take a smoke, Tophat and Billy Boy appear playing a game of cowboys. They begin shooting at each other furiously, and when neither falls to the ground, an argument ensues.)*

### TOPHAT

You're suppose to be dead, Billy Boy. I shot you ten times.

### BILLY BOY

But I shot you first!

### TOPHAT

*(insistently)* No you didn't! I shot you first.

### BILLY BOY

But I'm suppose to be faster than you.

### TOPHAT

What makes you say that?

### BILLY BOY

'Cause I'm Billy the Kid.

### TOPHAT

*(unimpressed)* But I'm Jesse James. And that makes me the fastest.

### BILLY BOY

Who says Jesse James was faster than Billy the Kid?

**TOPHAT**

Everybody knows that.

**BILLY BOY**

It's not true!

**TOPHAT**

Are you calling me a liar?!

**BILLY BOY**

You are if you say Jesse James is faster than Billy the Kid.

**TOPHAT**

That's what you think! *(Pushes Billy Boy, and the two boys begin wrestling each other to the ground. Grandpa Marcus rises quickly and pulls them apart.)*

**GRANDPA MARCUS**

Now, you two cowboys, just hold it a second. *(stands between them)* Fighting never settled anything. Especially when you are only playing.

**BILLY BOY**

But Tophat doesn't play fair, Grandpa Marcus. I shot him first.

**TOPHAT**

Yeah – but you missed. And then I shot you.

**GRANDPA MARCUS**

*(rubs forehead)* I see. Now why would Billy Boy miss?

**TOPHAT**

'Cause he's playing Billy the Kid, and I'm Jesse James.

---

## BILLY BOY

So!

## TOPHAT

So that makes me the best shot. *(looks at Grandpa Marcus)* Ain't that right, Grandpa Marcus?

## GRANDPA MARCUS

Well I hate to disappoint you, but I'm afraid – you're both wrong.

## BILLY BOY

*(surprised)* What you mean, Grandpa Marcus? It had to be one of them...unless you're thinking about Wild Bill Hickcock or Buffalo Bill.

## TOPHAT

Maybe he's thinking about Bat Masterson or Wyatt Earp.

## GRANDPA MARCUS

*(smiles)* No – I'm not thinking about none of those guys. Have you ever heard of Deadwood Dick?

## BILLY BOY

*(scratches his head)* Who's he?

## TOPHAT

Yeah...Grandpa Marcus...who's he?

## GRANDPA MARCUS

*(proudly)* Why, he was only the best all around cowboy that ever lived. Could do everything – ride bronco, rope cattle – and he was the best shot you ever laid eyes on.

**TOPHAT**

If he was that good – why ain't we ever heard of him?

**GRANDPA MARCUS**

Maybe because he was a Black man.

**TOPHAT**

A Black cowboy?!! You gotta be kiddin'...

**BILLY BOY**

Sure gotta be. Ain't never heard of no Black Cowboy.

**GRANDPA MARCUS**

Well, it's about time you did. Why don't you two cowboys come over here *(walks to his rocking chair and takes a seat),* and I'll tell you about some of the Black cowboys who helped to make the West. *(The boys flop on the ground next to him.)* Yes, there were a lot of Black cowboys in the old West. Most of them were ex-slaves who came out West just like the white folks to look for a better way of life. They did all the things white cowboys did – rope, ride bronco, take part in cattle drives, some were homesteaders, others were outlaws, and many of them could shoot and fight with the best. But the most famous of them all – at least many of the old timers will say – was Deadwood Dick, or Nat Love – that was his real name. *(The boys look attentive.)*

**BILLY BOY**

How did he get the name Deadwood Dick?

**GRANDPA MARCUS**

Well, there's different versions. When you become a legend in your own time – people have a tendency to change things a little.

**TOPHAT**

You mean they tell lies!

## GRANDPA MARCUS

No, not exactly. It's just that when you're a legend – it's hard for people to keep up with you. But to get back to your question – Deadwood Dick got his name from a town called Deadwood City in the Dakota Territory back in 1854. Now, Nat...er...Deadwood, grew up in Nashville, Tennessee. He was born a slave, but after the Civil War, he headed West to find his fortune. He was always a good rider and found no trouble getting a job as a cow puncher with the Duvall outfit in Abeline, Texas.

## TOPHAT

We want to hear about the fighting cowboys. The ones who carried guns.

## GRANDPA MARCUS

Cow punchers carried guns. And they had to do a lot of fighting to get their cattle to the market. Indians would attack them, and there was always the danger of outlaws stealing their herd.

## BILLY BOY

Like Billy the Kid!

## TOPHAT

Or Jesse James!

## GRANDPA MARCUS

Yep – those were a few. But none of them ever started a fight with Deadwood Dick. Not that he was like those two bad hombres. He seldom used his pistols. But when he did – he was quicker than grease lightnin'!

## BILLY BOY

*(rises and whips out his pistol)* You mean – quick as this?!

**TOPHAT**

*(also rises and whips out his pistol)* No, like this! Bang, bang!

**GRANDPA MARCUS**

Now you two boys just sit down. There was more to being a cowboy in those days than just knowing how to shoot a pistol. A man had to be tough in many ways. And the Black cowboys had to be even tougher. But they would also have fun, especially after completing a hard drive. And the place where they would have their fun would always be the old saloon. And there was no saloon in the entire West as famous as Cleopatra's Saloon. It was located in Boley, Oklahoma, an all-Black town, and on any night you would see some of the most famous Black cowboys in the territory there. *(Tophat and Billy Boy look with antici-pation as the scene ends.)*

### ACT ONE: SCENE TWO
### CLEOPATRA'S SALOON: AROUND 1870

*(Lights focus on OldTimer who stands at the bar while Bartender Joe wipes glasses.)*

**BARTENDER JOE**

Mighty quiet around here for a Friday evening – don't you think, Oldtimer?

**OLDTIMER**

Won't be for long, Bartender Joe.

**BARTENDER JOE**

You know something I don't know?

**OLDTIMER**

I always know something you don't know.

**BARTENDER JOE**

How do you know that?

**OLDTIMER**

Because I know.

**BARTENDER JOE**

Know what?!

**OLDTIMER**

What you don't know.

**BARTENDER JOE**

And just what is that?

**OLDTIMER**

If I told you – then you would know.

**BARTENDER JOE**

*(throws up his hands)* OK – I give up.

**OLDTIMER**

I knew you would. *(pulls out a pocket watch)* They should be coming in a few minutes.

**BARTENDER JOE**

Who?

**OLDTIMER**

*(pauses and looks at his watch)* The Duvall outfit. They have just completed a drive, and you know what that means.

**BARTENDER JOE**

I sure do. *(Begins putting glasses on the bar and filling them up as the Duvall Outfit come roaring into the saloon shouting "Whoopees" and singing the following song:)*

### THE CATTLE DRIVE

The drive was hard and rough
But now it's all over
The drive was long and tough
But now it's all over

No more sleeping on the trail
With the moon shining on your face
No more eating leftover food
That is really a disgrace

No more worryin' 'bout Indians
Sneaking up on you at night
No more chasing outlaws
Who are afraid to stand up and fight

No more riding on a horse
Sixteen hours a day
No more wearing dirty clothes
Now that we got our pay

*(The singing stops, and the men continue shouting "Whoopees!" and begin spreading out, some taking seats at tables, others standing at the bar. Deadwood Dick enters. He is dressed in fancy clothes and wears his holster around his leg. Everybody becomes quiet as he slowly walks over to the bar. The men at the bar move away.)*

**BARTENDER JOE**

*(nervously)* What'll it be, Deadwood? *(Deadwood doesn't answer. He looks around the room.)* A beer, perhaps? *(He still doesn't answer.)* Nice day, huh?

### DEADWOOD DICK
Stop the small talk, Joe. Have you seen Mississippi Mountain?

### BARTENDER JOE
*(Begins wiping the bar. The other cowboys remain quiet.)* No – er – ain't seen him, Deadwood. *(Deadwood gives him a hard stare.)* I mean, not today, that is.

### DEADWOOD DICK
When did you see him?!

### BARTENDER JOE
I – er, think it was – er, about two days ago. *(begins wiping glasses)*

### DEADWOOD DICK
Can't you be more specific?

### BARTENDER JOE
Yes – yes – it was two days ago. I remember for sure. He was with Texas Red and Arizona Slim.

### DEADWOOD DICK
Did he say when he'd be back?

### BARTENDER JOE
*(still nervous)* He didn't say, Deadwood. Really he didn't. *(drops a glass on the floor)*

### DEADWOOD DICK
Why are you so nervous, Joe?

### BARTENDER JOE
*(begins to stutter)* Me? I – er – er – I'm not nervous. *(drops another glass on the floor)*

---

## DEADWOOD DICK
I suppose I'll just have to wait for him. That is, if it's alright with you?

## BARTENDER JOE
Sure, Deadwood – er – er, that's just fine.

## DEADWOOD DICK
Good – I'll just stroll over to a table and play me some cards. *(walks over to a table as Bartender Joe shows a sign of relief)* Mind if I join you boys? *(takes a seat)*

## FIRST COWBOY
It be our pleasure, Deadwood. Ain't that right boys? *(The others nod their heads.)*

## SECOND COWBOY
Won't get no complaints out of me.

## THIRD COWBOY
Me either.

## FIRST COWBOY
What'll it be, Deadwood?

## DEADWOOD DICK
*(takes a pack of cards out of his pocket and drops them on the table)* Stud Poka – what else?! *(Begins to deal cards as the men simulate a card game. Cleopatra enters from the rear wearing a beautiful gown. She stops at the bar and begins to sing:)*

## <u>CLEOPATRA'S SALOON</u>

**Welcome to Cleopatra's Saloon, boys**
**Where you get only the best**

---

Ain't no other place like it
In the entire Southwest

You can go to San Antonio
But it won't be the same
You can go to El Paso
Or any other place you can name

You can go to Dodge City
Where you liable to get shot
You can go to Abilene
Where things are always hot

As long as you behave yourself
You can have a good time
Just remember to be gentlemen
And don't get out of line
For there's only one place in the West
Where you can feel free
And that's because your host
Is none other than me

*(The men begin to shout and cheer as Cleopatra walks over to Dead-wood Dick's table.)*


## CLEOPATRA

Well – well – if it ain't the pride of the West himself – Deadwood Dick. *(slaps him on the back)*


## DEADWOOD DICK

*(slightly perturbed)* Can't you see I'm playing cards, Cleopatra?!


## CLEOPATRA

*(smiles)* Of course I can, Deadwood. Do you think I'm blind?

**DEADWOOD DICK**

*(continues playing)* No, I don't think you're blind. But you are interfering with my concentration.

**CLEOPATRA**

*(spins around)* I thought you would like to concentrate on me instead. You haven't seen me in over two years.

**DEADWOOD DICK**

I've been on the trail most of the time.

**CLEOPATRA**

Well – you ain't on the trail now. Move aside, boys – me and Deadwood got things to talk over. *(The three cowboys reluctantly rise and move from the table, and she takes a seat.)*

**DEADWOOD DICK**

Now see what you've done! *(shows his cards)* And I was holding a royal flush.

**CLEOPATRA**

*(rises and places hands on hips)* If you really want to hold something royal – you'd hold me. They don't call me Cleopatra for nothing. *(begins to sing)*

**THEY CALL ME CLEOPATRA**

**They call me Cleopatra
'Cause I'm a Black queen
Named after a woman
Who was supreme**

**I'm not a European Lady
Don't confuse me with them
My folks are from Afrika**

**And we have our own beautiful women**

**Regardless of what history says**
**Cleopatra was Black like me**
**That's why I took her name**
**'Cause I'm also supreme**


### DEADWOOD DICK

So that's how you got your name.


### CLEOPATRA

*(sits at table)* Yep – that's how I got my name. Now tell me, Deadwood – what's this talk about you gunning after Mississippi Mountain?


### DEADWOOD DICK

Who said I'm gunning after Mississippi Mountain? I just want to see him.


### CLEOPATRA

Come on, Deadwood. I know better than that. You two never did like each other.


### DEADWOOD DICK

Well, we would never get married – if that's what you mean. But you ought to know that Deadwood Dick never goes gunning after anyone. I'm a cow puncher...Just a cow puncher. *(stands and begins to sing)*

### I'M A COW PUNCHER

**I'm just a cow puncher**
**Who likes to romp**
**And live among nature**
**'Cause that's my home**

I'm just a cow puncher
Trying to get by
Give me the open prairie
And a clear blue sky

I'm just a cow puncher
Who likes to rope steer
Or catch me a pony
That's fast as a deer

I'm just a cow puncher
Who likes to ride his horse
And stay out of trouble
'Cause that's my choice


### CLEOPATRA

And you're also the best shot in the West. They don't call you Deadwood Dick for nothing. Remember – I was in Deadwood City, Dakota when you got that name. They're still talking about those fifty straight bulls-eyes you shot that afternoon.


### DEADWOOD DICK

(trying to be modest) I was just lucky that day. But I don't draw my pistol unless I have to. I'm a peaceful man. (sits at table)


### CLEOPATRA

Well maybe you are. But that Mississippi Mountain is mean as they come. Why, I once saw him take ten shots in the rib cage, and he didn't wink one eye. Now, I run a respectable place, Deadwood. Ain't had a shooting here since Jesse James shot it out with One-Eye Slim. That was nearly three years ago.

**DEADWOOD DICK**

Don't you worry none. I ain't here to make no trouble. *(Mississippi Mountain enters and stands at the door. He is dressed in white and carries two pistols on his gun belt. His presence draws immediate silence, and everybody begins to move back.)*

**MISSISSIPPI MOUNTAIN**

*(in a harsh voice)* I'm looking for Deadwood Dick! Has anyone seen him!

**DEADWOOD DICK**

*(remains seated)* I've seen him, Mississippi Mountain. He's sitting right here.

**MISSISSIPPI MOUNTAIN**

*(moves toward Deadwood slowly)* Well, well, if it ain't Deadwood Dick himself. I thought the Apaches would have gotten you back in Dallas.

**DEADWOOD DICK**

*(smiles)* Almost did. But since it was only a hundred of them – they decided against it.

**MISSISSIPPI MOUNTAIN**

Still the braggart – huh, Deadwood! If you ask me, I think you're lying. *(Everyone takes cover, anticipating trouble.)*

**DEADWOOD DICK**

That's not too hospitable of you...calling me a liar.

**MISSISSIPPI MOUNTAIN**

*(touches his gunbelt)* Wanna make something of it!

---

### DEADWOOD DICK

*(rises slowly)* No use getting upset, now is it? *(Cleopatra moves away from table.)*

### MISSISSIPPI MOUNTAIN

Who's getting upset!

### DEADWOOD DICK

Judging by the way you talk – you are!

### MISSISSIPPI MOUNTAIN

*(begins to circle the room)* Judging by the way you're acting – I would say my talking is making you nervous. *(continues to circle the room with his hand on gun belt)*

### DEADWOOD DICK

I ain't never been nervous in my life, Mississippi Mountain. *(begins to circle the room also)*

### MISSISSIPPI MOUNTAIN

You are now.

### DEADWOOD DICK

Wanna bet!?

### MISSISSIPPI MOUNTAIN

Don't make sense betting, Deadwood.  When I get through with you – you won't be in any shape to pay off. *(stops)*

### DEADWOOD DICK

*(stops also)* Pretty big talk – comin' from a country boy.

### MISSISSIPPI MOUNTAIN

*(begins to move again in a wide circle)* Just cause I'm from Mississippi don't make me no country boy.

## DEADWOOD DICK

*(begins to circle in the opposite direction)* Then why do you act like one?

## MISSISSIPPI MOUNTAIN

Think you pretty smart – doncha!?

## DEADWOOD DICK

*(stops)* I can count to ten – if that's what you mean.

## MISSISSIPPI MOUNTAIN

*(stops and adjusts his gun belt)* Well, let's hear how well you can count now, Deadwood. 'Cause when you reach ten – you betta reach for your hardware. *(The two men stand facing each other.)* Well, why doncha start counting, Deadwood? Or has the cat got your tongue?

## DEADWOOD DICK

*(adjusts his gun belt also)* You're making a big mistake, Mississippi Mountain. *(long pause)* But if you insist – one – two – three – four – five – six – seven – eight – nine – *(Before they can draw their pistols, Oldtimer rushes into the saloon, shouting.)*

## OLDTIMER

Whoopee! Whoopee! Gold! Gold! They done struck gold in California! *(Deadwood Dick and Mississippi Mountain stare at each other as the others become jubilant and begin singing.)*

## GOLD! GOLD!

Gold, gold
We're off to get some gold
No more driving cattle
No more riding herd
Gonna get me a shovel and spade
And dig for some gold today

---

Gold, gold
Ain't got time for drinking
Ain't got time for dancing
Gonna get me a grubstake
And dig for some gold today

Come on, boys, we got to go
Come on, boys, let's get some gold

Gold, gold
There ain't nothing more beautiful
Than a rock that shines
Find one and everything is OK
So let's go and dig
And have a big pay day

*(They all begin to scramble and rush out of the saloon shouting. Mississippi Mountain, Deadwood Dick, Cleopatra and Bartender Joe remain.)*

### MISSISSIPPI MOUNTAIN

I suppose we gotta postpone this for another day, Deadwood. That gold sounds pretty good, and I could sure use me some of that yellow stuff. See you next time, Deadwood, you lucky stiff! *(departs in a hurry)*

### DEADWOOD DICK

*(laughs)* If you ask me, Cleopatra, Mississippi Mountain planned the whole thing.

### CLEOPATRA

Well, that might be, but what about you, Deadwood? Don't you want to find your fortune?

## DEADWOOD DICK

I told you – I'm a cow puncher, not a gold miner. And anyway, my treasure ain't buried beneath the ground. My treasure has two legs, nappy hair and a face as pretty as a flower.

## CLEOPATRA

Well, that sure ain't me. You must be talking about Lulu Belle. *(He nods his head.)* I thought so. Still stuck on her after all these years. Can't really blame you. She is a pretty looking thing. But where do you think you'll find her?

## DEADWOOD DICK

*(smiles)* Right here. The last time I saw her I told her I would be waiting in your saloon. So that's what I intend to do.

## CLEOPATRA

Taking a lot for granted, aren't you? Suppose she doesn't come.

## DEADWOOD DICK

*(takes a seat at a table and spreads out a pack of cards)* I stand a better chance finding my treasures here than trying to beat all those crazy goldminers trying to discover gold. And besides – she's worth much more. *(begins playing solitaire)*

## CLEOPATRA

That's a nice thing you said, Deadwood. You ain't such a tough guy after all. *(walks toward the bar as the scene ends)*


## ACT ONE: SCENE THREE
## FRONT PORCH: PRESENT

*(Lights come on the yard as Grandpa Marcus continues to talk to Billy Boy and Tophat.)*

## BILLY BOY
*(excitedly)* That Deadwood Dick must have been a bad dude.

## TOPHAT
I still think Jesse James is the baddest.

## GRANDPA MARCUS
Well, I don't know 'bout that. Wasn't easy being a Black cowboy back then. A Black man really had to prove himself to get any respect from white folks. And Deadwood Dick demanded respect from everybody. Why, whenever one of the famous Black cowboys came through Oklahoma in those days, they would always come to Boley just to see Deadwood. *(The boys become intense.)* Well, to get back to the story – most of the men in Boley had gone to California in search of gold. There's something 'bout gold that makes men want to give up almost everything – hoping to strike it rich. But Deadwood remained in Boley, Oklahoma at Cleopatra's Saloon and waited for his true love, Lulu Belle.

## CLEOPATRA'S SALOON: 1870

*(Lights come on Bartender Joe, who is mixing a drink. Deadwood enters wearily and takes a seat at the table.)*

## BARTENDER JOE
You look a bit tired, Deadwood. Maybe a cold beer is what you need. *(pours a beer and brings it to Deadwood)* Should make you feel better.

## DEADWOOD DICK
*(gulps down beer and wipes his mouth with hand)* Man, that was some mean horse. Do you hear me! That was one mean horse.

## BARTENDER JOE
If you said it was a mean horse – it must've been a mean horse.

---

## DEADWOOD DICK

I use to think a horse I broke in called Highwayman was the meanest horse I ever rode. But this horse was so mean – it took me nearly three hours just to get the saddle on his back.

## BARTENDER JOE

*(doubtful)* Are you sure it took three hours?

## DEADWOOD DICK

*(indignant)* Have you ever known me to tell a lie?

## BARTENDER JOE

Er – er – course not, Deadwood. Just seems like a long time.

## DEADWOOD DICK

You ain't heard the half of it. *(stands and begins to mimic riding a horse)* After I got the saddle on the critter, it took me another 12 hours to break him in.

## BARTENDER JOE

*(scratches his head)* Twelve hours?!!

## DEADWOOD DICK

*(continues to mimic)* Without getting off him once. *(Bartender Joe shows his skepticism again.)* When I first got on that critter, I held him pretty loose. Wanted him to feel relaxed, you know. But that critter kicked his hind legs so high I almost went ten feet in the air. *(Isaiah Dorman enters and observes Deadwood.)* But I didn't let that bother me none. For I got on that critter again and gave him a ride like he ain't never had before. *(contines his mimic)* Yes, I stayed on that critter and rode him til every ounce of meanness was out of his stubborn hide. Yeah – I showed him what a real cowboy was made of.

## ISAIAH DORMAN

*(in a hearty voice)* Yeah – sugar and spice and everything nice.

## DEADWOOD DICK

*(turns suddenly in surprise)* Why, if it ain't Isaiah Dorman – you son of a gun. *(The two men embrace each other.)* And just how is the best scout this side of the Red River? *(Bartender Joe goes back to the bar.)*

## ISAIAH DORMAN

*(smiles)* Correction – Deadwood, I'm the best scout on both sides of the Red River.

## DEADWOOD DICK

*(returns smile)* That's a matter of opinion. You know – I used to be pretty good at that scouting business myself at one time. Why, did I ever tell you about the time I was leading this troop of pony soldiers through the Badlands of Dakota? *(waits for a response but gets none)* It was in the middle of winter, and the snow was over six feet deep. *(makes gesture with hands)* Why, it was –

## ISAIAH DORMAN

*(holds up his hands)* If you don't mind, Deadwood – I would like to get me a cold beer and take a hot shower. *(takes a seat and motions to Bartender Joe for a beer)* Anyway – you told me that lie before.

## DEADWOOD DICK

*(indignant)* It wasn't a lie, Isaiah! It was the God's truth! *(begins singing)*

## <u>NEVER TOLD A LIE</u>

**I never told a lie**
**Once in my life**
**Even though sometimes**
**I may sound a little trite**

---

Now I'm not saying
I've never stretched the truth
Maybe I did once
In my youth

But the fact of the matter is
I don't have to lie
'Cause everything I do
Cannot be denied


### ISAIAH DORMAN

Still the braggart. But I must admit – you do have the guts to back up your crazy stories. *(Bartender Joe brings beer to table.)* Thank you, Joe. *(Joe goes back to bar.)*

### DEADWOOD DICK

What brings you to these parts anyway, Isaiah?

### ISAIAH DORMAN

I'm on my way to see Colonel Custer. He wants me to take him to the Little Big Horn.

### DEADWOOD DICK

Are you outta your mind! That's Sioux country!

### ISAIAH DORMAN

So it is.

### DEADWOOD DICK

And don't you know the Sioux are at war?

### ISAIAH DORMAN

*(confidently)* You forget – I grew up with the Sioux. And Chief Crazy Horse is my personal friend.

---

**DEADWOOD DICK**

It doesn't matter. If you lead Custer to them, you'll be their enemy.


**ISAIAH DORMAN**

But Custer only wants peace.


**DEADWOOD DICK**

That ain't what I heard.


**ISAIAH DORMAN**

What have you heard?


**DEADWOOD DICK**

That he's looking to get a reputation by killing Sioux.


**ISAIAH DORMAN**

*(smiles)* I admit ol' iron face likes publicity, but I don't think he's foolish enough to go into Sioux territory looking for trouble.


**DEADWOOD DICK**

Take my advice – and don't go. We ain't got no business fighting Indians.


**ISAIAH DORMAN**

It's my job, Deadwood. You know I ain't never reneged on a job.


**DEADWOOD DICK**

You ought to, this time. *(Cleopatra enters from rear door. Upon seeing Isaiah, she goes to him and kisses him on the face.)*


**CLEOPATRA**

Well, if it ain't the king of the scouts. It's nice seeing you, Isaiah.

**ISAIAH DORMAN**

*(blushes)* It's nice seeing you too, Cleopatra. But where is everybody?


**CLEOPATRA**

Didn't Deadwood tell you? They're off to California – looking for gold.


**ISAIAH DORMAN**

I should've known. Every town I've been to the past three months was empty. In fact, it's been quite peaceful. *(begins singing)*

### IT'S BEEN PEACEFUL

It's been quite peaceful
Since gold was found
The streets are empty
In every town

Why, when I was in Dodge City
Not a gun was shot
I didn't even see one drunk
Lying in the lot

And Laredo was so peaceful
The sheriff went on vacation
And Doc Holiday didn't have
Not even one patient

In Abilene the town was quiet
As a cemetery at night
And no one was in jail
'Cause there had been no fights

## CLEOPATRA

*(places hands on hips)* Well, if you ask me, I would rather have the shooting and fighting. This ain't good for my business, you know. If Deadwood Dick wasn't passing the time away waiting for Lulu Belle, this would almost be a ghost town.

## ISAIAH DORMAN

So you're still sweet on Lulu Belle.

## DEADWOOD DICK

Could be she's still sweet on me. *(The two men begin singing a duet.)*

## <u>COULD BE, BUT IS SHE?</u>

## ISAIAH DORMAN

**Could be, but is she
After all these years being apart
How do you know
She's still your sweetheart**

## DEADWOOD DICK

**Lovers need not be together
Every day and every night
If they still feel for each other
Everything can still be alright**

## ISAIAH DORMAN

**Could be, but is it
How do you know she still cares
When you ain't seen her
After all of these years**

---

**DEADWOOD DICK**

Well, I'll soon find out
'Cause I'm gonna stay right here
And wait for my Lulu Belle
Even if it takes all year


**CLEOPATRA**

Will you two stop it! If Deadwood Dick thinks Lulu Belle is still his girl – then let him! *(places her arm around Deadwood Dick's neck)* Of course, if she's not – there's always Cleopatra.


**ISAIAH DORMAN**

I'll drink to that. *(raises his glass as Oldtimer rushes in wearing only his longjohns)*


**OLDTIMER**

*(excitedly)* He's here! He's here! *(tries to catch his breath)*


**CLEOPATRA**

Take it easy, Old Man. And ain't you pretty silly wearing those longjohns. Where's your manners?


**OLDTIMER**

He...er...made me take my clothes off.


**ISAIAH DORMAN**

Who's he?


**OLDTIMER**

Him...er...er...it's him...


**DEADWOOD DICK**

Get hold of yourself. Now who are you talking about?

---

**OLDTIMER**

*(points toward door)* Er...er...Chero...Cherokee Bill. He's here.


**ISAIAH DORMAN**

Wonder what Cherokee Bill's doing round these parts? Isn't there a price on his head?


**DEADWOOD DICK**

*(smiles)* Thinking 'bout collecting it?


**ISAIAH DORMAN**

I'm no bounty hunter. I may not like the crazy hombre, but I have no personal quarrels with him.


**CLEOPATRA**

He's crazy alright. 'Bout the craziest man I ever did see. Trouble seems to follow him everywhere. *(A flurry of gunshots are heard outside.)* You see – it's started already. *(Cherokee Bill enters holding two pistols above his head. Oldtimer runs for cover, and Bartender Joe hides behind the bar. The others remain calm at the table.)*


**CHEROKEE BILL**

*(shoots in the air and begins singing)*


<u>**I'M CHEROKEE BILL**</u>


**I'm Cherokee Bill, the outlaw**
**The meanest man in the West**
**If anyone doesn't like it**
**He can take me to the test**

**I'm meaner than Billy the Kid**
**And Jesse James too**

---

There ain't no other outlaw
That can do what I do

*(begins shooting again)*

I've robbed banks in Cheyenne
Held up stage coaches in Abilene
I'm the meanest outlaw
That you've ever seen

I'm wanted in every state
And there's a bounty on my head
But no one messes with Cherokee Bill
'Cause they will end up dead

### CLEOPATRA

If you don't stop acting like a fool, Cherokee Bill – you'll wish you were dead!

### CHEROKEE BILL

*(laughs)* Now don't get upset, Cleopatra. I'm just having a little fun.

### CLEOPATRA

Take your fun someplace else! This is a respectable place!

### CHEROKEE BILL

*(puts his pistols in his holster)* You must be putting me on. You ain't never run a respectable place.

### DEADWOOD DICK

*(makes his presence felt)* You heard what the lady said, Cherokee Bill. Now why don't you stop acting like a little boy and do as Cleopatra said.

**CHEROKEE BILL**

Well, well, if it ain't old Deadwood Dick. And if I'm not mistaken, that's Isaiah Dorman next to you.

**ISAIAH DORMAN**

It's me alright, Cherokee Bill. And I see you're still acting like a fool.

**CHEROKEE BILL**

Watch your mouth, Isaiah. I don't like people calling me a fool.

**DEADWOOD DICK**

Then stop acting like one.

**CHEROKEE BILL**

That goes double for you, Deadwood. Or maybe you think you're the fastest gun in the West.

**DEADWOOD DICK**

I'm faster than you, Cherokee Bill. You should know that.

**CHEROKEE BILL**

I don't know nothing – unless you can prove it.

**DEADWOOD DICK**

I can.

**CHEROKEE BILL**

Are you sure?

**DEADWOOD DICK**

Yep, I'm sure. Dead sure.

**CHEROKEE BILL**

*(laughs)* Suppose you're wrong.

## DEADWOOD DICK

I'm not.

## CHEROKEE BILL

Pretty confident, huh?

## DEADWOOD DICK

Pretty confident, yes.

## CHEROKEE BILL

Think you can back it up?

## DEADWOOD DICK

I always back up what I say.

## CHEROKEE BILL

Always???

## DEADWOOD DICK

Always.

## ISAIAH DORMAN

Why don't you two stop trying to out psyche each other. There's a way to prove who's the best.

## CHEROKEE BILL

What's that?

## ISAIAH DORMAN

A shooting contest. We can go outside and have a shooting contest.

## CHEROKEE BILL

Alright with me.

## DEADWOOD DICK

Fine with me too.

## ISAIAH DORMAN

OK, I'll toss some silver dollars in the air and see how many each of you can hit. (Both men nod their heads and proceed to go outside. Cleopatra and Bartender Joe follow.)

## OUTSIDE SALOON: DAY

## ISAIAH DORMAN

Alright, Cherokee Bill – you'll be first. I'll throw up one silver dollar.

## CHEROKEE BILL

(looks at Deadwood Dick) Which pistol do you want me to use, Deadwood?

## DEADWOOD DICK

(smiles) Why don't you use both of them. You'll stand a better chance.

## ISAIAH DORMAN

Alright, go! (Throws coin in the air and Cherokee Bill whips out both pistols and fires at it. Bartender Joe retrieves the coin.)

## BARTENDER JOE

(inspects the coin) It's a bull's-eye!

## ISAIAH DORMAN

You're next, Deadwood.

## DEADWOOD DICK

(feels his pistol) Make it two coins, Isaiah. I need a little incentive.

---

## ISAIAH DORMAN

Alright! *(Throws two coins. Deadwood draws his pistol and shoots at them. Bartender Joe retrieves the coins.)*

## BARTENDER JOE

Two bull's-eyes!

## CHEROKEE BILL

Make it three coins the next time, Isaiah.

## ISAIAH DORMAN

As you wish. *(Tosses three coins in the air. Cherokee Bill draws his two pistols and shoots at them. Bartender Joe retrieves the coins.)*

## BARTENDER JOE

Three bull's-eyes!

## DEADWOOD DICK

Not bad, Cherokee Bill. You must been takin' lessons.

## CHEROKEE BILL

I'll be happy to give you a few, Deadwood. That is, if you care to admit that I'm the best.

## DEADWOOD DICK

*(looks at him and smiles)* Make it ten this time, Isaiah, so I can settle this matter once and for all.

## ISAIAH DORMAN

Are you out of your mind, Deadwood? You only got six bullets.

## CLEOPATRA

I think you're over doing it, Deadwood.

## CHEROKEE BILL

Who's the fool now! *(laughs)*

## DEADWOOD DICK

I said ten, Isaiah! Or do you want me to throw them up myself?

## ISAIAH DORMAN

OK, Deadwood – you asked for it. *(Tosses up ten coins. Deadwood quickly draws his pistol and begins shooting at them over his back. Bartender Joe retrieves the coins as everyone watches in suspense.)*

## BARTENDER JOE

*(holds coins in his hand and begins counting)* One bull's-eye, two bull's-eyes, three, four, five, six, seven, eight, nine. *(a long pause)* Ten bull's-eyes – God dang it, he did it! He did it! God dang it – he did it! *(Cleopatra goes and hugs Deadwood Dick as Cherokee Bill takes the coins from Bartender Joe and inspects them.)*

## ISAIAH DORMAN

I know exactly how you feel, Cherokee. Why, if I didn't see it with my own two eyes – I never would've believed it.

## CHEROKEE BILL

It must be some trick! The coins had holes in them, already.

## DEADWOOD DICK

*(disturbed)* If you feel that way...Suppose we use ten of your coins, Cherokee.

## CHEROKEE BILL

*(contemplates for a while)* Forget it! Anyway, I got to be going. Suppose to meet some of my boys in Dodge City. Got to be a trick to it, Deadwood. Just got to be...*(mumbles to himself as he departs)*

---

**CLEOPATRA**

Deadwood, I don't know how you did it, but you sure made him look like one big fool. *(They all laugh as the scene comes to an end.)*

## ACT TWO: SCENE ONE
## FRONT PORCH: PRESENT

*(The lights come on Grandpa Marcus, who is still seated in his rocking chair talking to Billy Boy and Tophat.)*

### BILLY BOY

*(doubtful)* Was Deadwood Dick really that fast, Grandpa Marcus?

### GRANDPA MARCUS

That's what my Grandpa use to tell me.

### TOPHAT

If he was that good, why isn't he as famous as Billy the Kid or Jesse James?

### GRANDPA MARCUS

There's many reasons, my boy, some of which you should already know. Remember, Deadwood Dick was Black – and white folks have never given us our due credit. It wasn't easy being a Black cowboy in those days. After the Civil War, those who left their plantations had nothing. No land, no job and very little money. So many of them went West, especially to Kansas and Oklahoma. Why, did you know Oklahoma almost became an all Black state? At one time it had more Black towns than any other state in the Union. That's what Boley, Oklahoma was – an all Black town.

### BILLY BOY

How long did Deadwood Dick have to wait for Lulu Belle?

### GRANDPA MARCUS

Well, as the story goes – he waited, and waited some more. Began drinking a lot too. Everyday he would come to Cleopatra's saloon, sit at the table and play solitare.

---

# CLEOPATRA'S SALOON: 1870

*(Lights come on Cleopatra who is talking to Bartender Joe at the bar. Deadwood Dick is seated at the table playing solitare.)*

## CLEOPATRA

I'm really worried about Deadwood. He doesn't seem to be interested in anything. Just sits and sits.

## BARTENDER JOE

And he's drinking a lot, too, Miss Cleopatra. That Lulu Belle sure must be something special – for him to be feeling so low.

## CLEOPATRA

Sometimes a woman can make you feel that way. *(begins singing)*

### <u>SOMETIMES A WOMAN</u>
**Sometimes a woman
Can make you feel blue
Make you feel
Nothing is true**

**Sometimes a woman
Can make your heart
Feel like it's almost
Falling apart**

**Sometimes a woman
Can make you sad
Sometimes a woman
Can make you glad**

**But if you really love her
With all your heart
She'll light up your life
Like one big star**

**BARTENDER JOE**

I suppose a woman like that is worth waiting for.

**CLEOPATRA**

You can say the same thing for a man like Deadwood Dick. Deep inside – he's 'bout the nicest guy you ever wanted to meet. *(A man and woman enter. They look weary and are dressed in frayed clothes. The woman falls to the floor, and Cleopatra rushes to her aid.)*

**CLEOPATRA**

*(kneels over woman and feels her forehead)* Get a towel, Joe! Hurry! She has a high fever. *(looks at man)* What happened, Mister?

**BEN**

*(nervously)* We been traveling for a long time, ma'am. Mostly on foot. My wife – she's pregnant.

**CLEOPATRA**

*(feels woman's stomach)* She sure is. And judging from the size of her stomach she's due any day. Don't you know a pregnant woman shouldn't be on her feet too long?!

**BEN**

Yes, ma'am. But we didn't have much choice. After our stagecoach broke down in Kansas – we had to make it on our own.

**CLEOPATRA**

No wonder she's exhausted. *(Bartender Joe returns with a wet towel, and Cleopatra begins to apply it to the woman's forehead.)* It's a wonder either of you are living. Fix up some food for them, Joe. *(looks at Ben)* Mister – what is your name?

**BEN**

My name is Ben...Ben Jones, ma'am. And my wife...she's Lillie.

## CLEOPATRA

*(looks at Deadwood, who continues to play solitaire)* Alright, Mr. Jones, give me a hand. If Deadwood wasn't in some type of trance I'd ask him to help. *(She and Ben carry Lillie and sit her at a table. She'll be alright in a few minutes.)*

## BEN

Mighty kind of you, Miss...er...

## CLEOPATRA

Cleopatra.

## BEN

Mighty kind of you to help us, Miss Cleopatra.

## CLEOPATRA

That's what we Black folks suppose to do, Ben. I ain't doin' nothin' special. *(Lillie begins to awaken.)*

## LILLIE

*(half dazed)* Where are we, Ben? What happened?

## BEN

*(places arm around her)* Everything is fine, dear – just fine. We're among friends. This here is Miss Cleopatra.

## LILLIE

*(smiles)* Thank you, ma'am.

## CLEOPATRA

Wouldn't want anything to happen to that baby of yours. *(Lillie smiles and shakes her head.)*

---

## BEN

*(proudly)* Sure wouldn't.  It'll be our first one.  And he'll be free too!

## CLEOPATRA

How do you know it's gonna be a boy, Ben?

## BEN

*(confidently)* It's gonna be a boy alright.  Can feel it in my bones.
And like I said, he's gonna be free.  *(begins singing)*

### HE'S GONNA BE FREE

He's gonna be free
He's gonna be free
No more working for Massa
He's gonna be free

No more pickin' cotton
Til your hands are red
No more breakin' your back
Til you're too sore to go to bed

No more saying "Yes, sir"
When you really don't mean it
No more bowing your head
And actin' like you ain't got sense

No more being a slave
We're thru with all of that
No more being a slave
Just because we're Black

## CLEOPATRA

*(claps her hands)* That's the only way to be, Ben. And that's why
we're trying to make Boley the best place for Black folks in the State

---

of Oklahoma. Why, some folks feel the whole state will be Black some day.

## LILLIE

That would suit us just fine. *(Bartender Joe appears with two plates of food and places them on the table.)*

## CLEOPATRA

Now you two just eat and relax. After you've finished, we'll discuss what to do with you next. *(Ben and Lillie show their thanks, and she strolls over to Deadwood's table.)* You could've at least said hello.

## DEADWOOD DICK

*(stops playing)* What good is my hello gonna do for them? What they need is a place to stay. *(reaches into his pocket and brings out a roll of bills)* Here – this should be enough to help them get on their feet. But don't you let them know I gave it to them.

## CLEOPATRA

*(hugs Deadwood and kisses him on the cheek)* I knew you had a tender heart. Let me get you a drink.

## DEADWOOD DICK

Make it two.

## CLEOPATRA

All you get from me is one. When Lulu Belle comes – I don't want her to find you passed out.

## DEADWOOD DICK

Do you really think she's coming?

## CLEOPATRA

*(tries to be convincing)* Sure, she's coming. A woman would be a fool not to come back to a heap of man like you. *(A white man enters*

*wearing a badge.)* Why, it's Marshall Wyatt Earp. *(Marshall Earp glances around.)* You're a pretty good distance from Dodge City – ain'tcha – Wyatt. No outlaws here.

### WYATT EARP

*(goes to Ben's and Lillie's table)* What about horse thieves! *(pulls out his pistol)* So you thought I wouldn't catch up with you! *(Ben and Lillie appear frightened.)*

### CLEOPATRA

Hold it there, Marshall Earp. You got your people mixed up. These are good law abiding citizens. And the lady is about to have a baby.

### WYATT EARP

Makes no difference, Cleopatra! The law is the law. And these two are horse thieves. Now rise gently, Mister! *(Ben rises with his hands up.)*

### LILLIE

*(rises and clings to Ben)* You can't take him away! He only did it for me. I was too tired to walk any more. Have a little mercy – please!

### CLEOPATRA

Is it true what your wife says, Ben?

### BEN

Yes, ma'am. But it's like she says – she would have died out there if I hadn't got her a horse. I intended to pay the owner for the trouble we caused him. *(looks at Wyatt Earp)* Please, Mister. Give me another chance.

### WYATT EARP

*(firmly)* That's for the judge to decide.

---

**DEADWOOD DICK**

*(rises suddenly)* I'll be the judge, Wyatt.

**WYATT EARP**

Are you trying to interfere with the law, Deadwood?

**DEADWOOD DICK**

If you want to call it that. As for me – I prefer to call it standing up for justice.

**WYATT EARP**

But the man is a horse thief. You heard him.

**DEADWOOD DICK**

If your wife was bearing a child and needed help – you'd be a horse thief too!

**WYATT EARP**

I've no choice. I'm a U.S. Marshall.

**DEADWOOD DICK**

Then get back to Dodge City and arrest some of those two-bit outlaws who live there! Or are you tired of shooting people in the back?

**WYATT EARP**

*(moves toward Deadwood as Ben, Lillie and Cleopatra watch)* Be careful of what you say, Deadwood. I've never shot a man who didn't deserve it.

**DEADWOOD DICK**

And neither have I, Wyatt.

## WYATT EARP

You mean you would draw on me to protect them? *(points at Ben and Lillie)*

## DEADWOOD DICK

They deserve a chance to be free. I was a slave once myself. I know what they gone through to get here. *(Bartender Joe appears unnoticed behind the bar with a shotgun.)*

## WYATT EARP

I know you are pretty fast, Deadwood. But I already got the drop on you.

## DEADWOOD DICK

It doesn't matter, Wyatt. I'm not gonna let you arrest this man.

## WYATT EARP

Don't push your luck, Deadwood. I ain't got no argument with you.

## DEADWOOD DICK

You got one now, Wyatt. *(Begins moving toward Wyatt Earp)*

## WYATT EARP

Take another step – and you'll be pushing up daisies.

## BARTENDER JOE

*(points shotgun at Wyatt)* You'll be the one pushing the daisies, Marshall Earp – if you don't drop that pistol.

## WYATT EARP

*(turns and looks at Bartender Joe nervously)* Do you know what you're doing! I am a United States Marshall.

---

### BARTENDER JOE

*(boastfully)* And I'm a United States Bartender. So that makes us even. Now my patience 'bout to run out....say in about three seconds. One – two – *(Wyatt Earp drops his pistol and Deadwood retrieves it.)*

### DEADWOOD DICK

Now why don't you get on your horse, Wyatt, and hightail it out of here.

### WYATT EARP

I won't forget this, Deadwood!

### DEADWOOD DICK

It's best you do, Wyatt. No use carrying a grudge over something like this. *(begins singing)*

### DO YOURSELF A FAVOR

Do yourself a favor
And try and be smart
Life is too short
To have vengeance in your heart

Don't hold a grudge
'Cause you don't always win
Everyone loses sometime
Even the best of men

I know you're a famous Marshall
With a reputation to keep
But that doesn't mean
You can't also be weak

So do yourself a favor
And forget the whole thing

Life is too short
To have vengeance on your brain

*(Wyatt Earp looks flabbergasted at everyone and then storms out of the saloon. Ben rushes to Deadwood's side.)*

**BEN**

Me and the Mrs. will always be indebted to you, Mr. Deadwood Dick.

**DEADWOOD DICK**

You don't owe me nothing, Ben. *(Lillie joins them.)*

**LILLIE**

Well, if our baby is a boy like Ben says he's gonna be – I'm gonna name him after you.

**DEADWOOD DICK**

That's mighty kind of you, ma'am. If you do – I would appreciate it if you would call him Nat Love. That's the name my mama gave me. *(Lillie smiles and nods her head as Bartender Joe and Cleopatra look on in delight as the scene ends.)*

## ACT THREE: SCENE ONE
## FRONT PORCH: PRESENT

*(Lights come on the yard as Grandpa Marcus continues to talk to Billy Boy and Tophat.)*

### BILLY BOY
Are you sure everything you told us about Deadwood Dick is true, Grandpa?

### TOPHAT
Yeah, for a guy I've never heard about – he sure did a lot.

### GRANDPA MARCUS
Well, one can never be absolutely sure about a legend. You see, a legend keeps getting bigger and bigger each generation. *(spreads his hands)* Sometimes things are exaggerated a little bit. But you can bet your bottom dollar – Deadwood Dick actually lived.

### BILLY BOY
*(excitedly)* Whatever happened to Lulu Belle?!

### TOPHAT
Yeah, I'm anxious to find out, too!

### GRANDPA MARCUS
Well – like I said – when you become a legend, certain facts get lost – and new facts come out. Now, the way my Poppa Gus told me, Deadwood Dick remained at Cleopatra's saloon and waited for her.

## CLEOPATRA'S SALOON: 1870

*(Lights go out and come up on saloon. Bartender Joe is sweeping the floor as Deadwood sits at the table playing solitaire. Cleopatra is behind the bar, and Bartender Joe begins singing.)*

## I MAY NOT BE A COWBOY

I may not be a cowboy
And ride the range at night
I may not be a cowboy
I have never been in a fight

I'm just a simple bartender
Who works for an honest day's pay
I do my job the best I can
and don't have much to say

I can't even ride a horse
Nor never shot a gun
I don't even play stud poka
Unless it's for fun

Yes, I may not be a cowboy
But the West is in my bones
And this is where I hope to stay
Because it is my home


### CLEOPATRA
We are all glad it's your home, Joe, ain't that right, Deadwood?
*(Deadwood nods his head and continues playing solitaire.)*

### BARTENDER JOE
What's wrong with Deadwood?

### CLEOPATRA
I suppose he's still brooding over Lulu Belle. And the massacre at
Little Big Horn didn't help either. He and Isaiah were real buddies.
Too bad he was killed.

---

**BARTENDER JOE**

Sure was a shame. That General Custer must have been a dang fool to ride into Sioux territory the way he did. Didn't he know Chief Crazy Horse was at war with all pony soldiers?

**CLEOPATRA**

Some people claim he did. But when a man is out to get a reputation – he'll do almost anything.

**BARTENDER JOE**

Just like Cherokee Bill. They hung him, you know.

**CLEOPATRA**

No, I didn't – don't suprise me none.

**BARTENDER JOE**

It was Judge Parker who did it. Tell me he done hung over 200 men. The hanging judge, they call him.

**CLEOPATRA**

Yeah, I've heard about him.

**BARTENDER JOE**

Do you think the hangings will ever stop, Miss Cleopatra?

**CLEOPATRA**

I don't know, Joe. It's not easy living out here. This is a rough country. Needs taming – like a wild mountain lion. And plenty of the people need taming, too. But I got my hopes, Joe – and I got my dreams. *(begins singing)*

## I GOT MY HOPES

I got my hopes
I got my dreams
That some day this country
Will be serene

No more outlaws
Romping about
No more gun fights
And high noon shootouts

I got my hopes
I got my dreams
That some day this country
Will be supreme

No more hangings
And Indian wars
No more killings
And silly quarrels

### BARTENDER JOE
That would suit me just fine. What do you say to that, Deadwood?

### DEADWOOD DICK
*(does not look up)* Sounds pretty good to me. May not be practical –
but the idea is alright. Maybe I could hang up my guns for good.

### CLEOPATRA
Why don't you, Deadwood? *(walks over to his table)*

### DEADWOOD DICK
I will – when I settle down.

**CLEOPATRA**

And when will that be?

**DEADWOOD DICK**

I don't reckon I really know.

**CLEOPATRA**

I do.

**DEADWOOD DICK**

You do?

**CLEOPATRA**

Yes – when Lulu Belle ever gets here.

**DEADWOOD DICK**

She'll be here alright.

**CLEOPATRA**

It's been over a year already. Why don't you forget her, Deadwood? She's not doing you no good this way. You can't drink whiskey and play solitaire the rest of your life.

**DEADWOOD DICK**

I can do what I want, Cleopatra. Remember – I'm Deadwood Dick.

**CLEOPATRA**

I know who you are. But I also know a man can't sit around brooding over a woman without something happening to him.

**DEADWOOD DICK**

Would that matter to you? *(turns and plays coy)* I'm not talking about myself. Just thought maybe you cared a little.

## CLEOPATRA

I care a whole lot – but you've never noticed! *(walks away with tears in her eyes)* Joe – is everything ready for tonight? *(wipes her eyes)*

## BARTENDER JOE

Just like you said, Miss Cleopatra. And it sure should be a nice dance. Since most of the men done come back from gold digging in California – they just been itching to put on their dancing shoes.

## CLEOPATRA

I'm glad to hear that. We need some excitement round here. *(looks at Deadwood)* Maybe it will break up the monotony.

## BARTENDER JOE

It'll do more than that, Miss Cleopatra. It'll wake up this whole town. I just can't wait.

## CLEOPATRA

*(smiles)* You don't have to, Joe. *(extends her hands)* We can begin right now. *(Bartender Joe takes Cleopatra's hands, and they whirl around as the scene ends.)*

## ACT THREE: SCENE TWO
## CLEOPATRA'S SALOON

*(The lights come on Cleopatra's Saloon which is filled with cowboys dancing with their girls. This scene should be choreographed with dances reminiscent of the period. Whenever possible, a fiddler or a guitarist should play authentic music. While everybody is dancing and enjoying themselves, Deadwood Dick reamins at his table playing solitaire. Cleopatra strolls over to him and extends her hand.)*

## CLEOPATRA

Come on, Deadwood. You used to be pretty good on your feet.

---

## DEADWOOD DICK

*(without looking up)* Don't feel like dancing.

## CLEOPATRA

*(smiles graciously)* You can try.

## DEADWOOD DICK

Like I said – I don't feel like dancing.

## CLEOPATRA

Alright – have it your way. Just because Lulu Belle isn't here doesn't mean you have to be a wallflower. *(Mississippi Mountain enters with Lulu Belle holding his arm. When they are seen, everybody stops dancing, and the music stops also. Cleopatra moves away from Deadwood who stares at them.)*

## MISSISSIPPI MOUNTAIN

What's wrong with everyone? I thought this was to be a celebration. *(Everyone moves away, anticipating trouble.)* Is that any way to welcome two newly weds!! *(Deadwood remains seated as Cleopatra approaches him and Lulu Belle.)*

## CLEOPATRA

*(suprised)* You mean – you two done got married?

## MISSISSIPPI MOUNTAIN

*(boastfully)* That's what I said. Ain't that right, Lulu Belle! *(She timidly nods her head.)* Now why don't everybody start dancing again looks at Deadwood)* – unless there's somebody here who don't approve of me and Lulu Belle getting married!

## CLEOPATRA

Why you come here to celebrate your marriage?

## MISSISSIPPI MOUNTAIN

*(looks at Deadwood)* If Deadwood can come here – then I reckon I can too. *(Lulu Belle stays close to his side.)*

## DEADWOOD DICK

*(still seated)* I didn't come here to celebrate, Mississippi Mountain.

## MISSISSIPPI MOUNTAIN

Then why are you here?

## DEADWOOD DICK

I was waiting to see Lulu Belle.

## MISSISSIPPI MOUNTAIN

Is that so? Suppose she don't want to see you?

## DEADWOOD DICK

*(rises slowly)* I'm sure she can speak for herself. Is that right Lulu Belle?

## LULU BELLE

*(hesitates and then speaks softly)* I don't mind, Deadwood. It's just that I didn't think you wanted to talk to me since I got married to Mississippi.

## DEADWOOD DICK

*(remains standing near the table as the crowd begins to sense trouble)* That shouldn't matter none – between old friends.

## MISSISSIPPI MOUNTAIN

Suppose it matters to me?

## CLEOPATRA

I don't want no trouble, Mississippi.

## LULU BELLE

Mississippi ain't gonna start no trouble. *(looks at him)* Are you, honey?

## MISSISSIPPI MOUNTAIN

That depends on Deadwood. He might be a bit jealous.

## DEADWOOD DICK

I may be a little disappointed, but I'm not jealous, Mississippi. Don't believe in fighting over a woman. In fact, I wish the both of you all the happiness in the world.

## LULU BELLE

That's mighty kind of you, Deadwood.

## DEADWOOD DICK

If Mississippi makes you happy, Lulu Belle – I'm glad for you. Ain't never been one to hold a grudge in my heart. *(begins singing)*

### I'M NOT THE KIND OF MAN

**I'm not the kind of man
To hold hatred in my heart
Even the best of friends
Sometimes have to part**

**I admit I'm disappointed
You're no longer my girl
But life must go on
In this big world**

**I will always treasure
My memories of you
They were some of the best moments
That I ever knew**

So as long as you're happy
Then I'm happy too

And all my good wishes
Go out to the two of you


### MISSISSIPPI MOUNTAIN
*(extends his hand to Deadwood)* I had you all wrong, Deadwood. You got a lot of class. Let's shake on it.


### DEADWOOD DICK
*(shakes Mississippi's hand)* You're not too bad yourself, Mississippi. *(The two men smile, and Mississippi embraces Lulu Belle.)*


### CLEOPATRA
Well, what's everybody standing around for? This is suppose to be a celebration – isn't it! *(The music starts, and everybody begins dancing again and having a good time.)* Well, Deadwood – what are you gonna do now?


### DEADWOOD DICK
Don't really know. Maybe I'll just pack my bags and drift away.


### CLEOPATRA
You don't have to do that. I'm sure there's a lot of women who would love to be your girl.


### DEADWOOD DICK
For instance....


### CLEOPATRA
*(looks around as the dancing continues)* Well –

---

## DEADWOOD DICK

Like I thought...You can't even name one.


## CLEOPATRA

*(blushes slightly)* That's not true, Deadwood. There's me.


## DEADWOOD DICK

You mean – you and me!!!


## CLEOPATRA

Why not?


## DEADWOOD DICK

'Cause you're like a sister to me.


## CLEOPATRA

That's not the way I feel about you.


## DEADWOOD DICK

And just how do you feel, Cleopatra?


## CLEOPATRA

*(smiles)* I feel like a real queen around you, Deadwood. That's how I feel. *(begins singing)*


## I FEEL LIKE A QUEEN

**I feel like a queen**
**Whenever you are near**
**My heart becomes heavy**
**If you listened, you'd hear**

**I feel like a queen**
**When you touch my hand**
**I feel good all inside**

Don't you understand

I feel like a woman
Floating on a cloud
If you were my man
I would really be proud

Yes, you make me feel
Like a beautiful queen
If only you knew
What you meant to me


### DEADWOOD DICK

*(holds her hand)* Are you sure you know what you're saying? *(She nods her head.)* Well, maybe we should give it a try. I mean – I always felt like a king myself. And a king should have a queen. *(She smiles and nods again.)* In that case, Cleopatra, I'll be your king – if you'll be my queen. *(smiles and begins singing)*

### <u>I'LL BE YOUR KING</u>

I'll be your king
If you'll be my queen
We'll be together
Just you and me

I'll be your king
And will build us a throne
Some place in the valley
That we can call our own

*(embraces Cleopatra and they begin singing a duet)*

### CLEOPATRA
Yes, I'll be your queen
If you'll be my king

---

We can get married
We don't need a ring

**DEADWOOD DICK**

Yes, I'll be your king
If you'll be my queen
And I know everything
Will be lovely and serene

**DEADWOOD & CLEOPATRA**

We'll be together
As king and queen
We'll be together
As king and queen

*(They continue to embrace and repeat the verses as everyone looks on and the scene ends.)*


**ACT THREE: SCENE THREE**
**FRONT PORCH: PRESENT**

*(Lights come on the yard as Grandpa Marcus continues to talk to Billy Boy and Tophat.)*

**BILLY BOY**

*(looks disappointed)* Is that the way it ends, Grandpa?

**GRANDPA MARCUS**

*(stretches)* Yep, that's the way it ends.

**TOPHAT**

And no one gets killed?

**GRANDPA MARCUS**

What's wrong with Deadwood and Cleopatra falling in love?

**BILLY BOY**

*(shrugs shoulders)* I don't know. Just don't seem right.

**TOPHAT**

Yeah – it should end with some action.

**GRANDPA MARCUS**

*(stands)* You see enough of that on television. It's time you two boys begin to think of something else.

**BILLY BOY**

Like what, Grandpa?

**TOPHAT**

Yeah – like what?

**GRANDPA MARCUS**

Well – like learning how to love and respect each other. There's enough violence in the world already. *(begins singing)*

## <u>LEARN TO LOVE EACH OTHER</u>

**There's enough violence in the world
People are fighting everywhere
What we need is plenty of love
And learn how to give and share**

**Learn how to love each other
Love your sister
Love your brother
Learn how to love each other
Love your father**

Love your mother

There's enough killing in the world
You see it in the streets and on TV
What we need is plenty of love
And learn how to live in harmony

There's enough tragedy in the world
It's happening everywhere
What we need is plenty of love
And learn how to care

*(They all hold hands as the ensemble appears and joins in the singing as the play comes to an end.)*

**THE END**

# ABOUT THE AUTHOR

USENI EUGENE PERKINS is a poet, playwright and social practitioner whose works have been widely published. His produced plays include *Image Makers, Professor J.B., The Murder of Steve Biko* and *The Last Phoenix*. He is also the editor of *Black Child Journal*. His social commentary on Black children, *Home Is a Dirty Street*, was cited by Lerone Bennet, Jr. as ". . .one of the most important books on the sociology of the streets since publication of *Black Metroplis*." Mr. Perkins was the recipient of a Chicago Community Trust Fellowship. He is the founder and president of the Association for the Positive Development of Black Youth. The Association consults on rites of passage, youth gangs, manhood training and family development.